WISDOM OF THE WORD

Bible Study Series

I0099102

2 Corinthians

Letters of Love and Admonition

Helen Silvey
Jeannie McCullough, Executive Editor

BEACON HILL PRESS
OF KANSAS CITY

Copyright 2006

by Beacon Hill Press of Kansas City and Wisdom of the Word

ISBN 083-412-243X

Printed in the United States of America

Cover Design: Darlene Filley

Library of Congress Cataloging-in-Publication Data
Silvey, Helen, 1931-
  2 Corinthians : letters of love and admonition / Helen Silvey ; Jeannie
 McCullough, executive editor.
    p. cm. — (Wisdom of the Word Bible study series)
  Includes bibliographical references.
  ISBN 0-8341-2243-X (pbk.)
  1. Bible. N.T. Corinthians, 2nd—Textbooks.   I. McCullough, Jeannie.
 II. Title. III. Title: Second Corinthians. IV. Series.
 BS2675.55.S55 2006
 227'.30071—dc22

   2006000147

10 9 8 7 6 5 4 3 2 1

Contents

About Wisdom of the Word   4

Introduction to 2 Corinthians   5

L E S S O N   1   7

L E S S O N   2   17

L E S S O N   3   27

L E S S O N   4   37

L E S S O N   5   47

L E S S O N   6   57

L E S S O N   7   67

L E S S O N   8   77

L E S S O N   9   85

L E S S O N   1 0   93

Notes   103

About Wisdom of the Word

Wisdom of the Word (W.O.W.) was founded in 1986 by Jeannie McCullough in Bethany, Oklahoma. It began as a weekly Bible study at Bethany First Church of the Nazarene. In the first year the study grew to over 400 members, and women from other churches and the community began joining. The local enrollment of Wisdom of the Word eventually exceeded 1,000 and has included men, women, and children of all ages and many denominations.

Wisdom of the Word has been an instrument in uniting the community of believers as well as reaching the unchurched and the lost. It is now ministering to thousands through videos and cassette tapes and other programs such as Children of the Word, prison ministries, and missions.

About the Name

W.O.W. began as "Women of the Word." Then when men began to join in the study with the women, the name was changed to "Wisdom of the Word," not only to retain the W.O.W. acronym but also to reflect the mission: to have our lives visibly changed by gaining wisdom from God's Word and responding in radical obedience to His voice.

About Jeannie McCullough

Jeannie McCullough was a pastor's wife until June 2004. She is also a mother and grandmother. Her life and ministry have taken her to Bethany, Oklahoma, where her husband, Mel, served as senior pastor of Bethany First Church of the Nazarene. In June 2004 he accepted the position of inaugural president of the Nazarene Foundation, located in Olathe, Kansas, near Kansas City. Since that time they have been in transition between Oklahoma City and Kansas City. Jeannie understands firsthand how radical obedience to God's Word can change a life.

Southern Nazarene University granted Jeannie an honorary doctorate in 1997. Due to her humor and honesty as well as her unique insights and application of the Scriptures in daily living, she is in great demand as a speaker throughout North America. Jeannie strives to be a "salt tablet" who will make others thirst for God's Word. As she has committed herself to being a student of the Word, God has given her many opportunities to share what He is teaching her.

About the Author

HELEN SILVEY is from a family of writers. She is a widow with four grown children. Helen has been a group leader for W.O.W. for many years and is very active in the life of Bethany, Oklahoma, First Church of the Nazarene.

Introduction to 2 Corinthians

Corinth was a wealthy cosmopolitan city, a seaport, and a great trading and commercial center located on a narrow isthmus in southern Greece. It was populated by Roman military veterans, merchants, Jews, and people from various lands to the east.

North-south traffic passed through Corinth by necessity, east-west traffic by choice. Because the journey by ship around the cape at the southern end of the isthmus was 202 miles of dangerous seas and high winds, most traders chose to cross the four miles of land across the isthmus through Corinth. Small ships were dragged out of the water, set on rollers, hauled across the land, and relaunched on the other side. Large ships had their cargo unloaded, carried across, and reloaded on a ship on the other side.[1]

Corinth was known for its wickedness and immorality. All sorts of vices and filth came in with the traders and sailors. It was a center of worship of many old Roman and Greek gods. Towering above the city was the hill of Acropolis where the temple of Aphrodite, goddess of love, was located with its 1,000 sacred prostitute priestesses. Each evening these prostitutes descended to ply their trade on the streets of Corinth. This was the culture out of which the new Corinthian Christians had come.

Paul stayed in Corinth 18 months, longer than in any other city except Ephesus. His first visit to Corinth is recorded in Acts 18:1-17. He apparently made two more visits (2 Corinthians 2:1, 3; 13:1-2) and received a visit while at Ephesus from members of the church at Corinth (1 Corinthians 16:17).

Paul's letters to the churches follow the standard style for that period, and 2 Corinthians is typical of this style:

- The greeting (1:1)
- A prayer for the people to whom it is written (1:2)
- Thanksgiving (1:3)
- The main body of the letter
- Final greetings (often including personal greetings from others) and a prayer that God would bless them (13:11-14)

Paul's letters were dictated to a secretary but often had a final greeting handwritten by Paul himself. They are not sermons or academic exercises that follow an outline point by point but are very personal letters, usually written to meet an immediate situation or problem. He often pours out his thoughts, one after another, sometimes in a somewhat disconnected manner. "It is just because Paul's letters were written to meet a threatening danger or a claimant need that they still throb with life. And it is because human need and human situations do not change that God speaks to us through them today."[2]

1 Corinthians was written from Ephesus in A.D. 55, 2 Corinthians probably about a year later. Some of Paul's correspondence with the church at Corinth has apparently been lost (or possibly is out of order). Bible scholars give this chronology of events:

- A previous letter (see 1 Corinthians 5:9). Most believe this letter was lost, but some believe the body of it might be found in 2 Corinthians 6:14—7:1.

As you begin each day, use this acrostic to help you study:

Wait for the Holy Spirit to teach you as you read His Word.

Obey what God instructs you to do.

Remember to praise God for insights and promises fulfilled.

Discover for yourself the incredible faithfulness of God!

- 1 Corinthians
- Paul may have made a difficult visit to Corinth in which matters became worse and in which he found himself the object of a painful attack (see 2 Corinthians 2:1, 3, 5; 7:12).
- A severe letter (see 2 Corinthians 2:4; 7:8). Most

Bible scholars believe that this letter has been lost, but some believe that it is 2 Corinthians 10—13. These chapters reflect Paul's hurt and heartbreak as he strongly defends his credentials, his integrity, and his apostolic authority. And so they believe that 2 Corinthians 1—9, which is positive and conciliatory, should follow 2 Corinthians 10—13.

2 Corinthians

■ A Study of 2 Corinthians 1:1—2:11

Appointed and Anointed with Grace and Peace

Read 2 Corinthians 1:1-2.

1. Who wrote this letter, and how did he further identify himself?

2. To whom was the letter written?

At the time this letter was written, Achaia encompassed the southern half of present-day Greece. (The northern half was Macedonia.) The letter was addressed not only to the church in Corinth, the capital city, but also to all the Christians in Achaia. This would have included the church in Cenchrea (Romans 16:1) and the Christians living in Athens (Acts 17:15, 22, 34), two prominent cities in Achaia. Apparently they were aware of the problems in the Corinthian church and probably affected by them as well.

The Greek word from which we get the word "apostle" means "to send." An apostle was one who had seen and heard the risen Lord, and had been commissioned and sent by Him, with the authority to speak for Him. False prophets in Corinth were opposing Paul and his teachings

and questioning the legitimacy of his apostleship, influencing some of these new Christians against Paul. Paul was reminding them that he was not speaking and teaching on his own authority but *as an apostle of Christ Jesus by the will of God.*

3. Record Christ's words in Luke 10:16 to those He appoints to be His workers.

Paul's apostleship had been accepted by the disciples in Jerusalem (Acts 9:26-28) and his message confirmed at the Council of Jerusalem (Acts 15:1-29).

4. Record 2 Corinthians 1:2.

God's grace always precedes His peace. To know His peace, we must experience His grace. We do not deserve it and cannot earn it. Grace is a gift of God through His Son, Jesus Christ.

2 Corinthians 9:6

Remember this: Whoever sows sparingly will also reap sparingly, and whoever sows generously will also reap generously.

5. Personalize and record the following:

   Romans 3:23-24

   Ephesians 1:7 (Read verses 1-8.)

   Ephesians 2:8

6. God not only provides saving grace but also blesses us with His keeping grace that sustains and strengthens us day by day, especially through the hard times, the trials and persecutions, the sorrows and disappointments. This is the grace Paul is referring to here. Record 2 Corinthians 12:9.

7. According to the following verses, what does God's keeping and sustaining grace do for us?

   1 Corinthians 1:4-5

   Hebrews 4:16

8. When we have experienced God's grace, we also experience His peace. As we grow in Christ, we experience this peace with others and within ourselves. Summarize the following verses:

   John 14:27

   Romans 5:1

   Romans 8:6

If you have accepted the gift of God's grace through faith in His Son, Jesus Christ, you have been appointed to witness to others (Matthew 28:18-20) through your obedient life and spoken testimony. And you will also receive the precious anointing of God's abiding grace and the peace, *which is far more wonderful than the human mind can understand* (Phil. 4:7, TLB).

DAY TWO

The God of All Comfort

Read 2 Corinthians 1:3-7.

1. By what titles does Paul refer to God?

2. Why does God comfort us in all our troubles?

3. What does comfort produce in those who are suffering (verse 6)?

Paul praises God for His compassion and His comfort in times of trouble. God's mercies are great and never-failing.

4. Record Lamentations 3:22.

Jesus said, *If you love me, obey me; and I will ask the Father and he will give you another Comforter, and he will never leave you. He is the Holy Spirit* (John 14: 16-17, TLB). When we are experiencing difficult circumstances, and God through His Holy Spirit comforts us, it does not mean that our troubles will just go away. God often comforts us by giving the strength, encouragement, and love we need to deal with our situation. "The more we suffer, the more comfort God gives us."[1]

5. Record the following verses.

Psalm 23:4

Psalm 145:8-9

Isaiah 43:2-3

God comforts us through His Word and His Spirit and often uses other believers to give us the encouragement we need. When we have received comfort, we are to pass it on to others. "We are not comforted to be comfortable but to be comforters."[2] Comfort is far more than mere sympathy. It is someone coming alongside you to provide support, encouragement, and strength. Those who have been through deep sorrow or trial know the right words to say and the comforting actions to take for those going through similar circumstances.

6. Make a note of a difficult time in your life when someone who had gone through a similar difficulty gave comfort to you.

Has an experience of yours enabled you to comfort someone who was suffering?

The sufferings of Christ refers to the trials we endure in Jesus' name because we are faithfully following God's will—suffering for righteousness's sake.

7. Read 1 Peter 4:12-16, 19, and summarize verses 16 and 19.

8. Record Matthew 5:10-11.

9. According to Matthew 5:12, why should we *rejoice and be glad* when we suffer because of righteousness?

As the sufferings increase, so does the supply of God's mercy and grace. *Let us then approach the throne of grace with confidence, so that we may receive mercy and find grace to help us in our time of need* (Hebrews 4:16).

Throughout the world Christians are allowing themselves to be persecuted and killed rather than denying Christ. Have you (or has someone you know) been cut off from your family, perhaps considered "dead," because you are a follower of Christ? Have you ever felt isolated or ridiculed in the workplace or school because you would not join in some un-Christlike activity? If you have endured suffering and trials for no reason except that you are a follower of Christ and you have experienced God's grace and comfort, be prepared to share with your group. It may be the word of encouragement someone needs. And don't forget to praise God, *the Father of compassion and the God of all comfort, who comforts us in all our troubles.*

MEMORY CHALLENGE

If our comfort to others is given sparingly, we will reap

_____. If it is given generously, we

will reap _____.

DAY THREE

Rely on God

Read 2 Corinthians 1:8-10.

1. How does Paul describe the way he and his companions felt as a result of the hardships they had suffered in Asia?

Paul had endured many trials and difficulties as he served in obedience to His Lord: he had been insulted, chased from town, beaten, imprisoned, and stoned. People had even tried to kill him.

Paul refers in this passage to some extreme hardship his companions and he had suffered recently in Asia. Whatever had been the cause of his suffering, he believed that there was no escape, that he would surely die. He was under pressure so severe that he felt it was *far beyond [his] ability to endure.* No person could save him; he could not save himself; his hope was in God alone.

God *does not willingly bring affliction or grief to the children of men* (Lamentations 3:33), but He does not always protect His children from trials and suffering. Sometimes He delivers us from trial; other times He allows the trial but walks with us. "The Arabs have a proverb, 'All sunshine makes a desert.' The danger of prosperity is that it encourages a false independence; it makes us think that we are able to handle life alone."[1] God wants us to learn, as Paul did, to rely on Him, to place our trust in Him.

No one enjoys trials or suffering, but during our trials we do tend to spend much more time in prayer and in God's Word. We identify with Abraham Lincoln, who said, "I have often been driven to my knees in prayer because I had nowhere else to go."[2]

2. On Day Two you recorded Psalm 23:4 and Isaiah 43:2. God gave us a promise found in each of these verses that we can rely on. What is it?

3. What do the following verses say that God will do for you if you put your trust in Him?

Psalm 9:9-10

Isaiah 41:10

Nahum 1:7

Isaiah 41:13

Romans 8:28

Jesus gave this wonderful promise: *In me you may have peace. In this world you will have trouble. But take heart! I have overcome the world* (John 16:33). We may not know what our tomorrows hold, but we can say with assurance that we know who holds our hand.

MEMORY CHALLENGE

Ask God to help you give (sow) more generously. Thank Him for His generous blessings.

4. Sometimes we suffer trials and persecutions because we are followers of Christ (refer to Day Two). What benefits do the following scriptures assure us?

Romans 5:3-4

2 Corinthians 4:17

1 Peter 1:6-7

1 Peter 5:10

If we rely on God when we are in the furnace of affliction and testing, God will shape and mold us, refine and purify us, and strengthen our faith. We will draw closer to God and grow more Christlike. And we will experience God's love, compassion, and comfort (2 Corinthians 1:3-4). When we have experienced the presence of the Lord walking with us through the fiery furnace, we develop an unshakeable confidence that God is very present in the midst of our trials. And that produces peace and freedom from fear—in the present trial and for the future.

5. Personalize and record the following verses:

Deuteronomy 31:8

DAY FOUR

Pray for Each Other

Read 2 Corinthians 1:10-11.

Pray for each other. . . . The power of a righteous [person] is powerful and effective (James 5:16).

1. According to today's scripture, what does Paul say God had done for him and will continue to do?

2. What help does Paul request from the church at Corinth?

3. What will be the result of answered prayer?

Paul requested prayer for himself and his companions in ministry. These brave missionaries faced dangers, hardships, and persecutions in their travels to spread the gospel of Jesus Christ. They needed the prayers of the church. Paul also knew that as the members of this troubled church prayed together, they would experience a greater sense of unity. Paul would have believed that "the [church] that prays together stays together."

One of the greatest gifts that we as members of the Body of Christ can give to one another is the gift of prayer. It is an honor and a privilege to be asked by someone to pray for him or her. And what a blessing and comfort to know that others are praying for us!

4. Explain in a few words how the truths in the following verses relate to today's lesson:

Ecclesiastes 4:9-12

Matthew 18:19-20

Romans 12:5

5. Record Galatians 6:2.

6. If you have experienced a time when the prayers of others changed the difficult circumstances of your life or that of a family member, share this answer to prayer with your group.

Lea was a college freshman, an accomplished pianist. She was dating the young man who is now her husband when she developed a strange swelling and severe pain in one of her fingers. She had the recommended surgery on the finger, but soon the pain and swelling reoccurred. A rheumatologist was consulted; the diagnosis was psoriatic arthritis, a form of arthritis that attacks various joints sporadically.

Lea was placed on a low dosage of the chemotherapy drug, Methotrexate. Regular blood tests had to be conducted to check for life-threatening side effects. The arthritis seemed to improve, but Lea was warned that if she should someday want to start a family, the medication would need to be discontinued months before she became pregnant.

Lea was married in August 1992. The young couple did not have health insurance at that time, and because the medication and necessary blood tests were very expensive, Lea tried to discontinue the medication but suffered flare-ups of crippling pain. Sometime the pain was so severe that she was unable to carry on her usual activities, walk without limping, or even get up without help.

Here is Lea's testimony:
> In the midst of these trials, God was so faithful to me, and I learned to depend on Him in very real ways. Although I hesitate to call these trials "suffering," I learned that in a mysterious sort of way, suffering is one of God's greatest blessings. I know that sounds strange, but when you are in the midst of suffering, you must depend on God so completely. Rather than dreading or begrudging these physical trials, with God's help I was able to thank Him and ask Him for His strength and endurance to get through them and to teach me what He wanted me to learn through my circumstances.

When the time came that we wanted to start our family, I had no choice but to get off the Methotrexate. These were probably the most difficult days of my life physically. On November 3, 1996, my 25th birthday, I received a very special letter from my dear friend Glaphré Gilliland. My parents and my husband and I all sat in my living room and read it together. God had spoken to her, directing her to ask a few people to pray and fast for me on November 4. . . .

The letter read as follows:
Dear Lea:

Because we believe in God's power and His love for you . . . because we believe in you and love you . . . on Monday, November 4, 1996, we will each be doing our own personal fasting and praying for you. We will be asking God to help your medicine be effective, to retard and stop the progression of the arthritis, and to release His healing within your body and begin recreating wholeness there.

In God's unique and perfect timing, it was exactly one year later that I became pregnant with our daughter, Emma. Pregnancy was physically a very good time for me. As many autoimmune conditions go and as my doctors had hoped, the arthritis virtually vanished for the whole nine months. But exactly nine days after Emma was born, the pain and inflammation reappeared. It was discouraging, though not unexpected. My husband and I made the decision for me not to go back on the Methotrexate at this time, and as an alternative, my doctor put me on steroids to try to keep the arthritis under control, though we knew this couldn't be a permanent solution.

After several busy months of taking care of a new baby . . . I was having my devotions one day and reflecting on the pain I used to deal with when God spoke to me in a very clear voice and said, "Do you not even realize that I'VE HEALED YOU?"

It was such an overwhelming realization! I couldn't even tell anyone about it for several days. Later, after sharing the news with my family and my doctor, I began to wean myself off the steroids. It wasn't very long before I was totally off the steroids and controlling the arthritis with only a very small dose of one anti-inflammatory medication.

A few months ago I was telling Glaphré that my days of such extreme pain seem to be a very distant memory. . . . Before Emma was born I remember thinking . . . *Maybe I shouldn't have children. Is it really fair to have a mom who can't run and play with you?* And yet, through my doubts and worries, God continued to be faithful!

After I got pregnant with our second daughter, Lily, the arthritis again totally vanished, and I was able to get off all medications. . . .

If this were the end of the story, it would certainly be incredible enough. But you know, God is always greater than we could ever hope or imagine! After Lily was born in January, I quietly counted as the days passed waiting for the arthritis to reappear. I guess I really thought that God had done enough by giving me two beautiful, healthy daughters and by just letting the disease be controlled with so little medication. After 18 days had passed, I cautiously commented to my husband and to my mom that I really had not had any pain to speak of.

Well, Lily is now a toddler, and I am still arthritis free! I don't know if the arthritis will ever come back, and you know what? It doesn't even matter! God has healed me! I truly believe that if it all were to come back tomorrow, it would not in any way take away from this miracle in my life. Our God is so good!

MEMORY CHALLENGE

If you are generous with your prayers for others, you will reap _____ blessings.

Stand Firm in Christ
Anointed, Sealed, and Guaranteed

Read 2 Corinthians 1:12-22.

1. Paul states that he has conducted himself in the world and with the Corinthians _____

   _____ _____ _____

   _____ _____ _____

   _____ _____ . . . not

   _____ _____ _____

   _____ but _____ _____

   _____ _____ .

2. In verse 20 what does Paul say about the many promises God has made?

False teachers had infiltrated the church at Corinth and caused the church to be divided into factions. They had attacked Paul's character and questioned his authority as an apostle. Paul begins now to defend himself, his ministry, and his message. He testifies that he has conducted himself not with deceit or hypocrisy but with holiness and godly sincerity, not according to worldly wisdom but relying on the wisdom that comes from the grace of God. His letters to them contain no hidden meanings; the message is clear and understandable.

Paul was accused of not keeping his word because he had not gone to Corinth after his visit to Macedonia as he had originally planned. (He explained the reason in 2 Corinthians 1:23—2:1.) Therefore, according to his accusers, Paul was untrustworthy, and the message he preached could not be trusted. So Paul reminded the Corinthians that all God's promises concerning the Messiah had been fulfilled in Jesus Christ, and it was through believing in the message of Christ that the people of Corinth had received God's grace.

3. According to 2 Corinthians 1:21-22, what four things had God done for Paul and the Corinthian Christians and does for all who accept Jesus Christ as Lord and Savior?

4. God establishes and empowers the believer; He makes us *stand firm in Christ*. Summarize the following verses:

   Romans 8:9

   Romans 8:37-39

   2 Thessalonians 3:3

5. Read Ephesians 6:10-18. What are we told that we must do in order to stand firm?

   List the parts of *the full armor of God*.

Paul assures all believers that God has anointed them and placed on them His seal of ownership. Old Testament kings, priests, and prophets were anointed with oil for God's service. Today God anoints those of us who belong to the royal priesthood of believers (1 Peter 2:9) with His Holy Spirit, who commissions, equips, and empowers us.

6. Summarize 1 John 2:26-27.

In former times, as a guarantee of their authenticity, letters were sealed with wax that was imprinted with an identifying mark. Legal documents today are often imprinted with an official seal. Ranchers brand their cattle to identify them as belonging to them. And God places His seal of ownership on His people; the presence of the Holy Spirit is the identifying mark of a true believer.

7. Jesus gave us this promise: *I will ask the Father, and he will give you another Counselor to be with you forever—the Spirit of truth. . . . You know him, for he lives with you and will be in you* (John 14:16-17).

Record the following verses:

1 Corinthians 2:12

1 John 4:13

8. *Since we live by the Spirit, let us keep in step with the Spirit* (Galatians 5:25). List the character traits (fruit) of the Spirit-filled life as recorded in Galatians 5:22-23.

9. God has also put His Spirit in the believers' hearts as a deposit, a guarantee of His promise of eternal life with Him in heaven. Summarize and personalize the following verses:

Romans 8:11

Ephesians 1:13-14

Titus 3:5-7

Thank You, Lord! Praise Your holy name!

MEMORY CHALLENGE

Fill in the blanks:

Whoever _____ _____ will also _____ _____, and whoever _____ _____ will also _____ _____.

DAY SIX

Forgive!

Read 2 Corinthians 1:23—2:11.

1. What reason did Paul give for not returning to Corinth as he had originally planned?

2. What did he hope he would accomplish by writing to them instead of visiting? (Refer to 2 Corinthians 13:10.)

3. Describe Paul's emotions as he wrote the earlier letter to the Corinthians (2:4).

4. Paul wrote that letter not to _____ _____ but to let them know _____ _____ _____ _____ _____ for them.

What reason did he give in 1 Corinthians 4:14 for writing the letter that is now 1 Corinthians?

5. Now that the transgressor had been punished and had repented, Paul instructed the church to do three things. According to 2:7-8, what were they?

6. What reason did Paul give for forgiving the person *for your sake* (2:10)?

Paul had sent Titus to Corinth in his place and had sent with him the severe letter that he, Paul, had written with such anguish. Titus had returned with the report that the Corinthians had been obedient in carrying out the discipline, and the person had repented (2 Corinthians 7:6-16). Some commentators believe this to be the immoral man of 1 Corinthians 5. Most, however, believe this individual, whether a member of the church or a visitor, had challenged Paul's authority as an apostle and possibly was the leader of a group opposing Paul. The Corinthian Christians had tolerated the sin, and it was this attitude that had caused Paul to write to them in such a severe manner.

There was apparently some division in the church concerning the punishment of this person; some had been unwilling to punish him, while others believed that he had not been punished enough. Paul tells them he agrees with the punishment but that now they must forgive this person, comfort him, and reaffirm their love for him. He does not want him to be overwhelmed by sorrow or by their disapproval and lack of acceptance. Satan could use the situation (1) to embitter and defeat the transgressor, (2) to cause division within the local Body of Christ, and thus (3) to destroy the influence of the church in the community.

7. Read Matthew 18:15-35. Record Peter's question in verse 21 and the answer Jesus gives in verse 22.

Explain in one sentence the spiritual lesson in this parable.

8. Summarize the following verses:

Matthew 6:14-15

Luke 17:3-4

Ephesians 4:32

Colossians 3:13

1 John 3:18

Churches too often are lax about punishing sinners in their fellowship. When *godly sorrow brings repentance* (2 Corinthians 7:10), churches should be forgiving and loving. The purpose of church discipline should be (1) repentance, (2) reconciliation, and (3) restoration. Examine your attitude toward the repentant sinner.

MEMORY CHALLENGE

Quote 2 Corinthians 9:6 from memory.

2 Corinthians

LESSON 2

■ A Study of 2 Corinthians 2:12—4:12

The Aroma of Christ

Read 2 Corinthians 2:12-17.

1. What reason did Paul give that he *still had no peace of mind*?

Apparently Paul had expected to meet Titus in Troas with news about how the church at Corinth had reacted to the letter written by Paul and delivered to them by Titus. This was the severe letter written *out of great distress and anguish of heart and with many tears* (2 Corinthians 2:4). Paul was concerned about the safety of Titus, who had been collecting money for the church at Jerusalem, and was so burdened about the situation at Corinth that he left Troas even though *the Lord had opened a door there* (verse 12) for ministry. He was able, however, to return to Troas and to stay for seven days on a later trip (Acts 20:6-11).

Paul now leaves his narrative of concern for Titus and the church at Corinth to reflect on the ministry to which God had called him and on his total dependence on God for its effectiveness. He returns to the story about Titus and the Corinthians in 2 Corinthians 7:5.

2. Read 2 Corinthians 7:5-7 and summarize verses 6-7.

3. According to 2:14, what does God spread everywhere through Paul and through us as followers of Christ?

4. What does Paul say believers are to God (2:15)?

5. To the one (who rejects Christ) we are _____ _____ _____ _____. To the other (the one who accepts the message of salvation) we are _____ _____ _____ _____ (verse 16).

6. Record Paul's question in 2 Corinthians 2:16.

   How did Paul answer his question? See 2 Corinthians 3:5.

In Paul's time, victorious Roman generals, accompanied by their soldiers, government officers, musicians, and their captives would march through the streets of Rome in a triumphal procession. Sometimes the parade would begin

2 Corinthians 9:7

Each man should give what he has decided in his heart to give, not reluctantly or under compulsion, for God loves a cheerful giver.

early in the morning and last far into the night. A general would ride in a chariot drawn by four horses. In front would be captives who would soon be freed to become Roman citizens. In the rear would be the captives who were to be executed.

Marching alongside the parade were priests carrying censors with burning incense to their gods. The smoke from the incense would drift over the parade; its perfume would be an aroma of life, joy, and triumph for the victors and for the captives who were to be freed. For the doomed captives, it was the aroma of death.

To Paul, preaching the good news of Jesus Christ was like being part of His triumphal entry. It is not clear whether Paul considered himself to be a victorious partner with Christ or whether he was implying that he was a willing captive of Christ. The meaning "is much the same either way. If a captive, the nature of the captivity is such that it is in the deepest sense also triumph for Paul—triumph in Christ because it is God who triumphs over him! The victory of the gospel is Christ's and the apostle is privileged to share in it."[1]

"The dearest thing to the heart of God is the death of his Son. The second dearest thing is when his children share that news with others."[2] When we share the good news of salvation through Jesus Christ, it is a fragrance pleasing to God and a sweet, life-giving aroma to those who accept Him, but it is the smell of death to those who reject Him.

7. Record the words of Jesus in John 15:22.

8. Read 1 Peter 2:6-8, and fill in the blanks:

The one who trusts in Jesus *(a chosen and precious cornerstone)* will _____ _____

_____ _____ _____ (verse 6). To those who do not believe, Jesus will be _____

_____ _____ _____

_____ _____ _____ and

_____ _____ _____

_____ _____ _____. They stum-ble because _____ _____ _____

_____ (verse 8).

"My name will be great among the nations, from the rising to the setting of the sun. In every place incense and pure offerings will be brought to my name, because my name will be great among the nations," says the LORD Almighty (Malachi 1:11).

DAY TWO

A Letter from Christ

Read 2 Corinthians 3, concentrating on verses 1-3.

1. Record 2 Corinthians 3:2.

A letter of recommendation to introduce a person and to confirm the person's character was a common custom at the time of Paul's ministry. Apparently the false apostles in the church at Corinth had brought recommendation letters with them and were also asking the Corinthians to recommend them to other churches. The letters may have been authentic recommendations from the faction in Jerusalem that opposed Paul (Acts 21:17-29), or they may have been forgeries. They provided acceptance, hospitality, the opportunity to speak and teach, and often financial gain for the bearer.

These false apostles evidently were challenging Paul's authority as an apostle and minister by asking why he had no letter of recommendation.

2. Paul was not denying the value of these introductory letters; he had written them himself for some of his coworkers. Read the following verses, and identify the person(s) for whom Paul wrote a letter of introduction and recommendation.

Romans 16:1-2

1 Corinthians 16:10-11

2 Corinthians 8:17

Colossians 4:7-8

Philemon 1:10-12

What Paul was asking was why he should need any recommendation to the Corinthian church that had been founded and established under his ministry. If they were doubting Paul's credentials as an apostle, weren't they actually denying their own salvation? It was, after all, through the message that Paul had preached that they had accepted Christ and were now believers. The Corinthian Christians themselves were the evidence that confirmed Paul's ministry, their Spirit-filled lives a letter of recommendation that could be observed and read by everyone.

3. Paul told the Corinthians that they were a *letter from*

   Christ, . . . written not with _____ *but with*

   _____ _____ _____ _____

   _____ _____, *not [carved] on tablets of*

   _____ *but on tablets of* _____

   _____ (2 Corinthians 3:3).

4. Record the words of the Lord in Ezekiel 11:19.

Does your life represent *a letter from Christ*, written on your heart by the Holy Spirit? Every person claiming to be a Christian is an advertisement—good or bad—for Christianity; the world judges Christ by the lives of those who claim to be His followers. Just as the changed lives of the Corinthian Christians confirmed the authenticity of Paul's message of the gospel, the evidence of the Holy Spirit in your life and

mine affirms the truth of the gospel of Jesus Christ. And it is the presence of the Holy Spirit in our lives that enables us to live the holy, righteous life that God commanded: *Be holy in all you do; for it is written: "Be holy, because I am holy"* (1 Peter 1:15-16). *For God did not call us to be impure, but to live a holy life* (1 Thessalonians 4:7).

5. What does God's Word tell us in the following verses about how to live a holy and righteous life so that we will be *a letter from Christ* to a lost and dying world?

   Matthew 5:16

   John 13:35

   Romans 6:11-12

   Philippians 2:14-15

   Ephesians 4:1-3

   1 John 2:6

1 John 3:6

6. Personalize Galatians 5:24-25.

We know that we live in him and he in us, because he has given us of his Spirit (1 John 4:13). *Live by the Spirit, and you will not gratify the desires of the sinful nature* (Galatians 5:16). *Then the way you live will always honor and please the Lord, and you will continually do good, kind things for others. All the while, you will learn to know God better and better* (Colossians 1:10, NLT).

> *O to be like Thee! O to be like Thee,*
> *Blessed Redeemer, pure as Thou art!*
> *Come in Thy sweetness; come in Thy fullness.*
> *Stamp Thine own image deep on my heart.*
> —Thomas O. Chisholm

> *Let the beauty of Jesus be seen in me—*
> *All His wonderful passion and purity!*
> *O Thou Spirit divine, All my nature refine*
> *Till the beauty of Jesus be seen in me.*
> —Albert Osborn

MEMORY CHALLENGE

What should each person give, according to 2 Corinthians 9:7?

DAY THREE

Life and Freedom in the Spirit

Read 2 Corinthians 3:4-18.

1. Who was the source of Paul's confidence?

   His competence as a minister came from _____.

2. Paul called himself a minister of *a new covenant—not of the letter but of the Spirit*. What do you think he meant by *the letter kills, but the Spirit gives life*?

3. Compare the glory of the old covenant of *the letter* with the glory of the new covenant of *the Spirit*.

4. Read Exodus 34:29-33. What was the cause of the radiance on Moses' face?

   According to 2 Corinthians 3:13, why did Moses put a veil over his face?

The law is not evil; it is *holy, righteous and good* (Romans 7:12), but self-justification through legalism—trying to follow the letter of the law but missing its true meaning—was harshly condemned by Jesus.

5. Read Matthew 23:23-33. What did Jesus call the teachers and Pharisees in verses 25 and 33?

No one but Jesus has ever been able to fulfill the law perfectly. Trying to be saved by keeping the Old Testament laws will lead only to failure, condemnation, and death. The law makes us realize our sins and shows us how to obey God but provides no help to comply. Forgiveness comes only through the mercy and grace of God when we believe in Jesus Christ.

But now we have been released from the law, for we died with Christ, and we are no longer captive to its power. Now we can really serve God, not in the old way by obeying the letter of the law, but in the new way, by the Spirit (Romans 7:6, NLT).

6. It is only the presence of the Holy Spirit in our lives that enables us to live a righteous life. Read Romans 8:1-4, and record verses 1-2.

The false teachers in Corinth, called "Judaizers," were insisting that the Gentile Christians in Corinth had to follow certain Jewish laws in order to be saved. So Paul was comparing here the differences between the old covenant of the "letter" and the new covenant of the Spirit. The ministry of the law had its glory but required continual sacrifices for forgiveness. The ministry of the Spirit is far more glorious, for it brings righteousness through the once-and-for-all sacrifice of Jesus Christ on the Cross.

Well then, why was the law given? It was given to show people how guilty they are. But this system of law was to last only until the coming of the child to whom God's promise was made. . . . Until faith in Christ was shown to us as the way of becoming right with God, we were guarded by the law. We were kept in protective custody, so to speak, until we could put our faith in the coming Savior. Let me put it another way. The law was our guardian and teacher to lead us until Christ came. So now, through faith in Christ, we are made right with God. But now that faith in Christ has come, we no longer need the law as our guardian. So you are all children of God through faith in Christ Jesus (Galatians 3:19, 23-26, NLT).

7. What does 2 Corinthians 3:17 tell us about the Spirit?

8. Does that freedom mean that you as a Christian are able to live in any manner and do anything you please? Record or summarize the following verses:

Romans 6:15-16

Romans 8:9

Galatians 5:13, 16

*Once I was bound by sin's galling fetters;
    Chained like a slave, I struggled in vain.
But I received a glorious freedom
    When Jesus broke my fetters in twain.*

*Glorious freedom! Wonderful freedom!
    No more in chains of sin I repine!
Jesus, the glorious Emancipator—
    Now and forever He shall be mine.*
                                        —Haldor Lillenas

9. According to 2 Corinthians 3:18, in what way is the Lord transforming the believers who *reflect the Lord's glory?*

All of us have had the veil removed so that we can be mirrors that brightly reflect the glory of the Lord. And as the Spirit of the Lord works within us, we become more and more like him and reflect his glory even more (3:18, NLT).

MEMORY CHALLENGE

What does God love?

The God of This Age

Read 2 Corinthians 4:1-4.

1. What did Paul say he had renounced and did not do?

2. To whom is the gospel veiled?

According to 2 Corinthians 3:16, when is the veil removed?

3. What has *the god of this age* done to unbelievers?

Paul continued to defend his ministry, the ministry of the Spirit (2 Corinthians 3:6). He assured the Corinthians that he had not watered down the message to make it more acceptable, nor had he manipulated or distorted the Word of God for his own benefit.

Paul had already implied that the false teachers in Corinth had peddled *the word of God for profit* (2 Corinthians 2:17). First-century peddlers were often accused of adding water to their wines and of using false weights for their own gain,

so Paul had made a strong accusation of dishonesty against those false teachers. They had corrupted and distorted the Word of God by mixing it with their own ideas and opinions or by diluting its message.

Sadly, God's truth is still being manipulated, altered, and watered down today by people who claim to preach and teach God's message. I heard a man claiming to be a minister of the gospel say on television recently that to insist that Jesus Christ is the only way to God (refer to John 14:5-6) is "narrow-minded bigotry."

4. Give one or two examples of God's Word being distorted, adulterated, or diluted in our world today.

Paul told these Corinthians once again that he had always proclaimed the Word of God with honesty and straightforward simplicity. If it was not understood, it was due to the heart condition of the hearer. The gospel of Jesus Christ is veiled to those who are perishing; they can't understand, because they refuse to believe.

5. Record 1 Corinthians 1:18.

6. Who is *the god of this age* who *has blinded the minds of unbelievers* (2 Corinthians 4:4), the one Jesus called *the prince of this world* (John 12:31; 14:30; 16:11)?

7. What do we learn about the god of this age from the following verses?

Job 1:7

Luke 8:11-12 (Read verses 4-18.)

Ephesians 2:2

1 Peter 5:8

Those who reject Christ have made Satan their god, whether they realize it or not. Even if they don't intend to serve or worship Satan, he controls and uses them. "Unless they come to Christ in faith, they have no choice but to obey Satan. There is no middle ground; people either belong to God and obey him, or they live under Satan's control."[1]

Satan's lordship is limited by God and it is temporary (Revelation 20:10), but it is very real in this evil age. It is a mistake to give him too much credit; he will flee if you resist (James 4:7), and he has no control over Christ (John 14:30). But Satan is alive and active in our world. Those who deny his existence are false prophets; God's Word confirms Satan's presence and his activity. He continues to blind the minds of unbelievers to prevent them from seeing the light of the gospel; he still seeks to draw a veil of error and confusion over the eyes of the believer.

If your sins have not been forgiven and you have not yielded your life to Christ, your life is under the control of Satan—and you are powerless to resist him. Unless you turn to Christ and give your life to Him, you are lost.

But faithful, obedient Christian, you do not need to greatly fear Satan. Do not neglect God's Word; hide it in your heart so that you *might not sin against [him]* (Psalm 119:11). *Do not give the devil a foothold* (Ephesians 4:27). *Be strong in the Lord and in his mighty power. Put on the full armor of God so that you can take your stand against the devil's schemes* (Ephesians 6:10-11). And always remember that *the Lord is faithful, and he will strengthen and protect you from the evil one* (2 Thessalonians 3:3). *You, dear children, are from God and have overcome [Satan], because the one who is in you is greater than the one who is in the world* (1 John 4:4).

Thank You, precious Jesus!

A mighty Fortress is our God,
A Bulwark never failing;
Our Helper He, amid the flood
Of mortal ills prevailing.
For still our ancient foe
Doth seek to work us woe;
His craft and pow'r are great,
And armed with cruel hate,
On earth is not his equal.

Did we in our own strength confide,
Our striving would be losing;
Were not the right Man on our side,
The Man of God's own choosing.
Dost ask who that may be?
Christ Jesus—it is He;
Lord Sabaoth, His name;
From age to age the same;
And He must win the battle.

And tho' this world, with devils filled,
Should threaten to undo us,
We will not fear, for God hath willed
His truth to triumph through us.
The prince of darkness grim—
We tremble not for him.
His rage we can endure,
For, lo, his doom is sure;
One little word shall fell him.

That word above all earthly pow'rs.
No thanks to them, abideth;
The Spirit and the gifts are ours
Thro' Him who with us sideth
Let goods and kindred go—
This mortal life also.
The body they may kill;
God's truth abideth still.
His kingdom is forever.

—Martin Luther

MEMORY CHALLENGE

God loves a cheerful giver. He does not want us to give

_____ or _____ _____.

DAY FIVE

Let Light Shine Out of Darkness

Read 2 Corinthians 4:4-6.

1. Why are unbelievers unable to see *the light of the gospel of the glory of Christ*?

2. How does Paul describe Christ in verse 4?

3. Jesus said, *I and the Father are one. . . . Anyone who has seen me has seen the Father* (John 10:30; 14:9). What do the following verses tell us about Jesus Christ as *the image of God*?

   John 1:18

   Colossians 2:9

Hebrews 1:3

No one can see God the Father (1 Timothy 6:16), but His Son Jesus reveals Him to us. Paul was saying to us, "Look at Jesus Christ! And there you will see the glory of God come to earth in a form that [we] can understand."[1] When a person looks at Jesus, he or she sees the One who sent Him (John 12:45).

4. Record God's words in 2 Corinthians 4:6.

When God created the earth, He said, *"Let there be light," and there was light* shining into the darkness of the physical world (Genesis 1:3). God sent His Son, Jesus, to be the light that would pierce and illuminate the spiritual darkness.

5. Read Isaiah 9:2 and Matthew 4:12-16, and record verse 16 of Matthew 4.

6. What did Jesus say about himself in the following verses?

   John 8:12

   John 12:46

This is the message we have heard from him and declare to you: God is light; in him there is no darkness at all. If we claim to have fellowship with him yet walk in darkness, we lie. . . . But if we walk in the light as he is in the light, we have fellowship with one another, and the blood of Jesus, his Son, purifies us from all sin (1 John 1:5-7).

Are you walking in *the light of the knowledge of the glory of God in the face of Christ* (2 Corinthians 4:6)?

MEMORY CHALLENGE

Fill in the blanks:

Each man should _____ what he has _____ in his _____ to give, not _____ or _____ _____, for God loves _____ _____ _____.

2 Corinthians 9:7

DAY SIX

Jars of Clay

Read 2 Corinthians 4:7-12.

1. What reason did Paul give that the treasure was in *jars of clay*?

2. Contrast Paul's trials with his deliverances.

   Example: Hard pressed but not crushed

Paul suffered persecutions, trials, imprisonment, physical danger, misunderstandings, afflictions, and personal attacks (11:23-27). He was sometimes discouraged but never defeated. God had delivered him from difficulties (1:10) and comforted him in all his troubles (2:14).

3. What did Paul say that he and all Christians carry around in their bodies?

   For what reason?

4. Record the following verses:

   2 Timothy 2:11-12

   Galatians 2:20

Clay jars were the most common vessels used in the ancient world. They had many uses: for eating, drinking, cooking, and storing food and oil. They were cheap, prone to leaking, very fragile, and would chip and break easily. Most were not particularly attractive, but they served their purpose.

Paul used these simple clay jars as a metaphor for those who love and serve God. We may feel weak and inadequate. We may be chipped, cracked, or broken. But God has entrusted to us this most precious treasure—the message of the incomparable glory of Jesus Christ and salvation through faith in Him. Christ is able to use our weaknesses, sufferings, disappointments, and trials as opportunities to demonstrate His power and presence—in us and through us—to others.

5. How did Paul feel about his weakness and God's grace and power? See 2 Corinthians 12:9-10.

This weakness Paul refers to is not about sin or vice or a character defect that you can change (such as overeating or impatience) but rather any trial or limitation that you have no power to change. Your limitations may be physical, emotional, intellectual, or talent-wise.[1] We may feel discouraged and inadequate because of the weakness—the chips and cracks—in our lives, but 2 Corinthians 4:7 teaches us that God can use us despite our human imperfections. "A person's flaws, scars, chips, and cracks allow the presence of an all-sufficient God to leak out. . . . Many will see Christ in you and be drawn to him because they relate more easily to someone who isn't perfect."[2]

It is when we humbly acknowledge our weakness that we are most motivated to be in God's Word, seek His presence daily, and fully place our trust in Him. Then God is able to demonstrate His *all-surpassing power* through us and make our efforts to live for Christ and to share the treasure of His gospel effective and life-changing. Sometimes it is through our brokenness that Christ is able to shine His light into the darkness. (See Judges 7:2.)

6. The Bible gives many examples of weak but yielded human vessels used by God to accomplish His purposes. List the names of some.

Lord, I am just a jar of clay. I have cracks, I am weak and powerless, yet You have entrusted to me this precious treasure. I need Your strength and Your power. Use my weaknesses, my trials and disappointments for Your glory. Work through me so that I might be an effective vessel for Your service. Mold me and use me, Lord. You are the Potter; I am the clay. In Your name I pray. Amen.

MEMORY CHALLENGE

Quote 2 Corinthians 9:7 from memory.

2 Corinthians

LESSON 3

■ A Study of 2 Corinthians 4:13—6:2

Renewal in the Present, Resurrection in the Future

Read 2 Corinthians 4:13-16 and Psalm 116.

1. What did Paul say *is written*?

Paul was quoting from Psalm 116:10. The author of Psalm 116 was overcome by trouble and sorrow, yet in the midst of his affliction he proclaimed his faith and confidence in the Lord and gave praise and thanksgiving for God's protection and mercy.

2. Select a verse from Psalm 116 that expresses your thoughts today, and record it.

3. What do you think might be the reason Paul identified himself with the thoughts expressed in Psalm 116?

4. What did Paul have faith to believe (2 Corinthians 4:14)?

5. Paul had suffered greatly to proclaim the gospel. According to verse 15, how did his faithful ministry benefit the Corinthians and bring glory to God?

6. Paul stated verse 16 that *we do not lose heart*. Where else in this chapter do you find these same words?

What was Paul referring to as *this ministry*? (For help with your answer, review 2 Corinthians 3:6.)

2 Corinthians 9:8

God is able to make all grace abound to you, so that in all things at all times, having all that you need, you will abound in every good work.

7. Paul had met the resurrected Lord in an encounter on the road to Damascus (Acts 9:3-7) and was confident that God *will also raise us with Jesus* (2 Corinthians 4:14). List the order of events that will take place when Christ returns, according to 1 Thessalonians 4:16-17.

8. *Outwardly we are wasting away* (2 Corinthians 4:16). What is taking place in the believer inwardly?

If Christ does not return first, our human bodies, these fragile *jars of clay*, will eventually die and return to dust. We face a continual decaying process from birth until the end of our earthly life. But if you are a faithful believer who belongs to Christ, you are promised inward renewal day by day through the ministry of the Holy Spirit as you are continually *being transformed into his likeness with ever-increasing glory* (2 Corinthians 3:18).

9. Read the following verses, and answer (with a word or two) what is required of us if we are to receive inward daily renewal:

Psalm 119:105 and Romans 15:4

Romans 12:12 (last phrase) and Philippians 4:6

John 14:15 and James 1:22

10. In what ways does the Lord provide renewal for the believer according to the following verses? (Limit your answers to as few words as possible.)

Isaiah 58:11

John 14:27

Ephesians 1:19

Hebrews 4:16

What will God give us according to this week's Memory Challenge (2 Corinthians 9:8)?

11. 1 Peter 3:12 promises us that *the eyes of the Lord are on the righteous and his ears are attentive to their prayer.* Personalize the promises in Isaiah 40:29.

Whatever pain or trial you might be experiencing, *do not lose heart.* Allow the inner strength from the Holy Spirit and the resurrection power of Christ to renew and strengthen you day by day. *May the God of hope fill you with all joy and peace as you trust in him, so that you may overflow with hope by the power of the Holy Spirit* (Romans 15:13).

The glorious truth of the hope we have in Christ Jesus compels us to join the psalmist and proclaim, *Praise the Lord* (Psalm 116:19).

May [the Lord] strengthen your hearts so that you will be blameless and holy in the presence of our God and Father when our Lord Jesus comes with all his holy ones (1 Thessalonians 3:13).

We Live by Faith

Read 2 Corinthians 4:16—5:8.

1. Paul said, *We do not lose heart* (4:16). What did he say we are achieving that far outweighs any troubles that we might be experiencing in serving Christ?

2. We are not to fix our eyes on *what is _____.* Why?

   We should instead fix our eyes on *what is _____.* Why?

3. How must we live in order to be able to fix our eyes on *what is unseen* (4:18), according to 2 Corinthians 5:7?

   How does Hebrews 11:1 explain faith?

4. In the *New Century Version*, 2 Corinthians 5:7 reads as follows: *We live by what we believe, not by what we can see.* Hebrews 11:1 says, *Faith means being sure of the things we hope for and knowing that something is real even if we do not see it.* List two or three elements of your Christian beliefs that in faith you firmly believe but that you cannot see physically.

We know that when these bodies of ours are taken down like tents and folded away, they will be replaced by resurrection bodies in heaven—God-made, not handmade—and we'll never have to relocate our "tents" again. Sometimes we can hardly wait to move—and so we cry out in frustration. Compared to what's coming, living conditions around here seem like a stopover in an unfurnished shack, and we're tired of it! We've been given a glimpse of the real thing, our true home, our resurrection bodies! (2 Corinthians 5:1-4, TM).

Many scriptures teach that our souls go to be with Christ immediately at the time of death. Jesus answered the questions of the Sadducees—who did not believe in resurrection—with these words: *About the resurrection of the dead—have you not read what God has said to you, "I am the God of Abraham, the God of Isaac, and the God of Jacob"? He is not the God of the dead but of the living* (Matthew 22:32). Moses and Elijah appeared on the mountain and talked to Jesus in the presence of Peter, James, and John (Matthew 17:1-8), and Jesus assured the believing criminal on the cross, *I tell you the truth, today you will be with me in paradise* (Luke 23:43).

Several of her children were present in the room when my grandmother died. She roused from a semiconscious state long enough to say, "There's Jesus at the foot of the bed! Do you see Him?" Her eyes then fixed on that spot, she reached up with her hands, and she left her family and went to be with the Savior she had served so faithfully. Not one of her children doubted that she had truly seen Jesus come to take her spirit to be with Him. That doesn't always happen when a Christian dies, but what a wonderful confirmation of *Today you will be with me in paradise.*

Most if not all of the New Testament writers had seen the resurrected Christ. And there was also a firm belief among all of them that when Jesus returns there will be a resurrection of the bodies of believers. The Greeks, however, did not believe in a bodily resurrection; only the soul, they believed, would enter eternity. Some of the Corinthian believers were teaching that there would be no bodily resurrection of the dead (1 Corinthians 15:12, 35). But Paul told them that *Just as there are natural bodies, so also there are spiritual bodies* (1 Corinthians 15:44, NLT).

Jesus told His followers that *A time is coming when all who are in their graves will hear his voice and come out— those who have done good will rise to live, and those who have done evil will rise to be condemned* (John 5:28-29). *The Lord himself,* said Paul, *will come down from heaven . . . and the dead in Christ will rise first* (1 Thessalonians 4:16), and Jesus Christ *will transform our lowly bodies so that they will be like his glorious body* (Philippians 3:21). "Although these new spiritual bodies will somehow be associated with our old physical bodies (Romans 8:23), they will be of an entirely different nature"—imperishable, glorious, immortal, and perfect (1 Corinthians 15:42-44).[1]

5. Read 1 Corinthians 15:35-44. How is the resurrection body compared to the mortal body in verses 42-44?

6. Paul said, *As long as we are at home in the body we are away from the Lord* (2 Corinthians 5:6). Read Philippians 1:21-24, and record verse 21. Is this your testimony?

Which did Paul say he would prefer (2 Corinthians 5:8)?

7. Paul was *torn between the two* (Phil. 1:23). Have you ever experienced similar feelings? Explain.

We believers may now be *at home in the body* rather than in heaven with the Lord, but the Holy Spirit dwells with us. His presence in our lives gives us a foretaste, as well as the promise, of the joy and glory of what is to come. And until that day when we are *at home with the Lord*, God gives us this glorious promise: *Those who hope in the Lord will renew their strength. They will soar on wings like eagles; they will run and not grow weary, they will walk and not be faint* (Isaiah 40:31).

MEMORY CHALLENGE

What does 2 Corinthians 9:8 say that God is able to do?

DAY THREE

Our Goal: To Please Him

Read 2 Corinthians 5:8-10.

1. Where will every Christian someday have to appear?

2. What will he or she receive there?

The *judgment seat of Christ* is not the final judgment (Revelation 20:11-15), when the dead will stand before the throne of God and the unsaved will be judged. At the *judgment seat of Christ* only believers will appear. It will not be judgment for sin; our sins have been forgiven, covered by the atoning blood of Jesus Christ. Believers will be judged for the way they have lived the Christian life.

We cannot earn salvation. We are not justified—saved—by our works, but *justified freely by his grace through the redemption that came by Christ Jesus* (Romans 3:24). But our actions, thoughts, and deeds will be evaluated, and we will be rewarded or will suffer loss in heaven accordingly. We will be judged by our faithfulness and our behavior toward others. We will be answerable to God for our moral purity, financial integrity, compassionate works, and even whether we have been teachable and have demonstrated humility.

3. Record the following verses:

Romans 14:12

Hebrews 4:13

4. What does 1 Corinthians 4:5 say that the Lord will *bring to light . . . and will expose* when He comes?

"How pleasing [we] will be when 'at home with the Lord' cannot be separated from how pleasing [we are] now 'at home in the body.'"[1] It was Paul's goal to please the Lord (2 Corinthians 5:9), and it needs to be the goal of every believer. The real evidence of our belief is how we act; if we have placed our faith in Christ, our desire is to live our lives to please Him.

5. Why did Paul say he prayed for the Colossians to have *the knowledge of [God's] will through all spiritual wisdom and understanding* (Colossians 1:9)? See Colossians 1:10.

6. Record Galatians 1:10.

7. Read Colossians 3:1-10. List the things that the Christian must *put to death* to be pleasing to Christ when He appears (verses 5, 8-9).

8. Is it enough just to *put to death . . . whatever belongs to your earthly nature*? See Colossians 3:5. Record James 2:17 (after the first phrase).

God has created us for a life of good deeds, which he has already prepared for us to do (Ephesians 2:10, TEV). "You're not saved *by* service, but you are saved *for* service. . . . We don't serve God out of guilt or fear or even duty, but out of joy and deep gratitude for what he's done for us. . . . We owe him our lives. Through salvation our past has been forgiven, our present is given meaning, and our future is secured. . . . Our loving service to others shows that we are

truly saved. . . . A saved heart is one that wants to serve. . . . We are healed to help others. We are blessed to be a blessing. We are saved to serve, not to sit around and wait for heaven."[2]

When I stand before the judgment seat of Christ, I pray that I might hear Him say, *Well done, good and faithful servant! . . . Come and share our master's happiness* (Matthew 25:21).

MEMORY CHALLENGE

Why does God *make all grace abound to you*?

A New Creation

Read 2 Corinthians 5:11-17.

1. According to verse 11, what reason did Paul give for trying *to persuade men*?

2. Paul stated that he was giving the Corinthians *an opportunity to take pride in us*. For what reason?

3. What *compels* Paul in his ministry?

4. Record Paul's words that describe anyone who is in Christ (verse 17).

Paul continued to defend himself and his ministry. His reverence for the Lord and the love of Christ compelled him to preach an honest gospel, trying to persuade people to accept God's offer of reconciliation to himself through Christ (verse 18).

Apparently Paul's critics in Corinth had accused him of being out of his mind. "The real enthusiast always runs the risk of seeming crazy to lukewarm people . . . Paul knew that there was a time for calm, sensible conduct, and he knew, too, that there was a time for the conduct which to the world looks mad. He was prepared to follow either for the sake of Christ and of men."[1] The false preachers who peddled the word for profit (2:17) were mostly concerned with what could be seen as worldly success—wealth and popularity. Paul's motivation was to honor God by *setting forth the truth plainly* (4:2).

Christ died for all—for me and for you—that we might have life. And *those who live should no longer live for themselves but for him who died for them and was raised again* (5:15). Are you living for Him?

5. Read Colossians 3:1-17. Summarize how we should live *as God's chosen people* (verse 12) according to verses 12-17.

In 2 Corinthians 5:17 we learn that *If anyone is in Christ, he is a new creation; the old has gone, the new has come!* Colossians 3:10 tells us that if we are in Christ, we *have put on the new self, which is being renewed in knowledge in the image of its Creator.* "We are not reformed, rehabilitated, or reeducated—we are recreated (new creations), living in vital union with Christ (Colossians 2:6-7). At conversion we are not merely turning over a new leaf; we are beginning a new life under a new Master."[2]

Last Sunday night at my church we had the privilege of hearing the baptism testimony of one who experienced drugs, alcohol, crime, and gang activity in his former life. The man who stood before us that night was *a new creation* in Christ Jesus; the old man was gone. As he read his testimony and told of the transformation in his life and in his family and of his determination to live for Jesus, the light of Christ's love shone clearly on his face.

I first accepted Christ at the age of seven, but there were stumbles and falls during my teen years. Yes, I kept up the pretense of living for Christ, and, no, I was never involved in drugs or alcohol or crime. My sins were gossip, a critical spirit, an unloving attitude, and neglect of God's Word. I did not spend time with Him in prayer, praise, and devotion. My old self was just as sinful in God's eyes as the old self of the man who gave that baptism testimony. I asked for forgiveness and recommitted my life to God in my early 20s, but even today, decades later, my new self still needs the presence and power of the Holy Spirit to correct me and to perform an attitude check when needed. And I must ask for forgiveness when I fail. But praise God—I, too, am *a new creation* in Christ Jesus, and my desire is to live for Him!

Search me, O God, and know my heart; test me and know my thoughts. Point out anything in me that offends you, and lead me along the path of everlasting life (Psalm 139:23-24, NLT).

God is able to make all grace abound to you, so that in

_____ _____ *at* _____ _____,

having _____ _____ _____

_____ , . . .

2 Corinthians 9:8

DAY FIVE

The Ministry of Reconciliation

Read 2 Corinthians 5:16-20.

1. In what way did Paul say he no longer regarded others (verse 16)?

What do you think Paul meant when he said that he once regarded Christ this way?

2. How has God *reconciled us to himself*?

3. What ministry has God given to anyone who is in Christ?

4. Record the message of reconciliation as stated in Ephesians 2:13.

5. Read 1 John 1:5-9. What does the blood of Jesus do for us?

Record 1 John 1:9.

Before Paul was confronted by the risen Christ on the road to Damascus (Acts 9:1-5), he had regarded Jesus as a humiliated, beaten, and crucified imposter, a messianic pretender with little education and cursed by God (Deuteronomy 21:23; Galatians 3:13). In that encounter on the Damascus road, Christ revealed himself to Paul as the promised Messiah of Israel, the Son of God, and Paul then recognized Jesus as the Suffering Servant of Isaiah 53.

6. Record Isaiah 53:3.

"Reconciliation implies an estrangement which has been overcome, so that happy relations are again possible for the estranged. . . . Men by disobedience and indifference have made impossible a true fellowship with God; the hindrance to this fellowship must be removed; with the removal, fellowship is again established—and this is reconciliation."[1]

In the Old Testament, reconciliation took place when the people offered their sacrifices. From Paul we learn that under the new covenant, "The sacrifice is not made by the sinner—it is made on his behalf by another; and the new life comes about because by faith the sinner sees the sacrifice as made on his behalf. Moreover, it is God who provides the sacrifice, and thereby takes the initiative in seeking reconciliation. . . . When His appeal through Christ evokes from sinful men repentance, faith, and love, reconciliation is accomplished."[2]

We also rejoice in God through our Lord Jesus Christ, through whom we have now received reconciliation (Romans 5:11).

7. Read Romans 3:22-26.

How do we receive righteousness from God?

Who has sinned, according to verse 23?

According to verse 25, why did God send Jesus as a sacrifice of atonement?

8. Personalize a summary of Colossians 1:21-23.

Paul reminds us that because of this reconciliation with God, which we Christians enjoy, we must be ambassadors for Christ. An ambassador is a "representative appointed by one country or government to represent it in another."[3] As believers, *our citizenship is in heaven* and we represent *a Savior from there, the Lord Jesus Christ* (Philippians 3:20). We have been given an awesome and important responsibility—to allow God, through us, to appeal to a lost world to accept the reconciliation to himself that He offers and that we believers have accepted from Him.

Paul stated that he no longer regarded people from a worldly view. We are to view others from God's perspective, not to evaluate them in regard to race, social background, or economic status. Christ died for all (2 Corinthians 5:15).

9. Read James 2:1-10. Explain in one sentence what that passage says to you about your attitude and conduct toward others.

How have you regarded others—from a worldly view or from God's perspective? If you have regarded others as the world does, ask God to forgive you and to place His holy love for others into your heart.

God reconciled Paul to himself and gave him *the ministry of reconciliation* (2 Corinthians 5:18). Are you a *new creation in Christ* (verse 17)? If you are, God *has committed to [you] the message of reconciliation* (verse 19), through the example of the life you have lived for Christ and through the word of your testimony of what Christ means to you and has done for you.

MEMORY CHALLENGE

Let God's *grace abound to you, so that in all things at all times, having all that you need,* you can share with someone today the message of reconciliation.

DAY SIX

Now Is the Day of Salvation

Read 2 Corinthians 5:20—6:2.

As Christ's ambassador, Paul urged the people in the church at Corinth to be reconciled to God. As Christ's ambassador, every believer should feel this urgency to share the good news of God's offer of reconciliation to Him through faith in Christ Jesus.

God made him who had no sin to be sin for us (2 Corinthians 5:21). Jesus Christ was sinless. Isaiah had prophesied (53:9) that the Messiah would do no violence, nor would there be any deceit in his mouth. Peter referred to Christ as *a lamb without blemish or defect* (1 Peter 1:19).

1. In John 8:29 what reason does Jesus give for His Father always being with Him?

2. Personalize a summary of Hebrews 4:14-15.

God made him . . . to be sin for us (2 Corinthians 5:21). Jesus Christ became a curse for us (Galatians 3:13). He took our place; He bore the consequences of our sins, exchanging our sin for His righteousness. Christ was sinless but bore our sin at His crucifixion. When we accept Him as Savior, He fills us with His righteousness. This is what is meant by Christ's atonement for sin. "God offers to trade his righteousness for our sin—something of immeasurable worth for something completely worthless."[1] "At-one-ment": at one with Christ.

3. Read aloud Isaiah 53:3-12. Record a phrase that is especially meaningful to you.

Write down some of our thoughts and feelings as you read this passage.

4. What does Paul urge in 2 Corinthians 6:1?

What do you think he means?

Commentators have explained several ways by which a person might take God's grace in vain. Some see it as the unbeliever who ignores God's appeal. The saving work of Jesus on the Cross is available and sufficient for everyone, but to receive it we must believe. When we realize the terrible price Christ paid for our salvation, how can we turn our backs on Him and refuse to accept the offer?

However, this most likely refers to those who have believed but don't take God's grace seriously enough to live up to the holy life it demands. How can we accept God's amazing grace and then neglect to read His Word, spend time with Him, and mature as a Christian? How can we accept God's grace and then deny Jesus by a disobedient, fruitless life? "When God gives men all his grace and they take their own foolish way and frustrate that grace which might have recreated them, once again Christ is crucified and the heart of God is broken."[2]

If you have not accepted this gift of grace or have not lived the holy life it demands, *We urge you, as though Christ himself were here pleading with you, "Be reconciled to God!"* (2 Corinthians 5:20, NLT).

5. God has freely given us His grace through Christ Jesus. From the following verses, what must you do to accept this offer and be saved?

Deuteronomy 4:29

Proverbs 28:13

Isaiah 55:7

Matthew 4:17; Acts 3:19

John 5:24; 11:25

If we confess our sins, he is faithful and just and will forgive us our sins and purify us from all unrighteousness (1 John 1:9).

> *Just as I am, without one plea*
> *But that Thy blood was shed for me,*
> *And that Thou bidd'st me come to Thee,*
> *O Lamb of God, I come! I come!*
>
> *Just as I am, and waiting not*
> *To rid my soul of one dark blot,*
> *To Thee whose blood can cleanse each spot,*
> *O Lamb of God, I come! I come!*
>
> *Just as I am, tho' tossed about*
> *With many a conflict, many a doubt,*
> *Fightings and fears within, without,*
> *O Lamb of God, I come! I come!*
>
> *Just as I am—Thou wilt receive,*
> *Wilt welcome, pardon, cleanse, relieve.*
> *Because Thy promise I believe,*
> *O Lamb of God, I come! I come!*
>
> *Just as I am! Thy love unknown*
> *Hath broken every barrier down.*
> *Now to be Thine, yea, Thine alone,*
> *O Lamb of God, I come! I come!*
>
> —Charlotte Elliott

MEMORY CHALLENGE

Read 2 Corinthians 9:8 aloud several times. See if you can write it from memory.

It's not complicated. Believe in Christ. Seek Him with all your heart and soul. Confess your sins, repent, and forsake your wicked ways.

Paul finishes this passage on reconciliation by quoting Isaiah 49:8 and then tells us, *Now is the time of God's favor, now is the day of salvation* (2 Corinthians 6:2).

6. When is the best time to seek the Lord, according to Isaiah 55:6?

That time is now! "The devil's time is always tomorrow: God's time is always today."[3]

7. Prayerfully record Psalm 51:1-2.

2 Corinthians

■ A Study of 2 Corinthians 6:3-18

DAY ONE

"Put No Stumbling Block"

Read 2 Corinthians 6:3-18, concentrating on verse 3.

1. Why did Paul say he was careful not to be a *stumbling block*?

Paul continued to defend himself from the accusations leveled at him and his ministry. He assured the Corinthians once again that he always was careful as a minister of the gospel of Jesus Christ to consider how his actions might affect his listeners.

2. Paul had already defended his message. What did Paul say about what he speaks in 1 Corinthians 2:13?

3. Paul also knew that a minister must be extremely careful about his or her personal behavior so that it could not be used as an excuse to reject the message. Of what did Paul boast in 2 Corinthians 1:12?

As I prepared this lesson, evangelist Billy Graham was conducting an evangelistic crusade in Oklahoma City. Here are excerpts from just two of the many complimentary articles published in *The Daily Oklahoman*. Fortunately, these could be written about most ministers; sadly, they cannot be said of all.

During more than 50 years of ministry, the evangelist has preached to more than 210 million people in 185 countries and territories. . . . Along the way, he has led hundreds of thousands of people to decide to live their lives for Christ.

And he has done it, always, with class. While some evangelists have proven to be phonies, undone by sex or money scandals, and while some . . . priests have been exposed as sexual predators, Graham has, by all accounts, practiced what he's preached.

Honest. Gentle. Humble. Authentic. Christlike. They were words used by friends and associates to describe Billy Graham.[1]

For 60 years, Graham has walked upright through the briar patch of public scrutiny. In this day of media ready to devour all who even barely stumble, Graham remains unscathed by scandal. He has not succumbed to sins of the finances or the flesh, which have taken down many a man of God. . . .

The best witnesses—for Jesus Christ or anyone else—are made not from fame but from substance. And that includes Graham, whose chief weapon in spreading the gospel is not the words he says but the life he lives. . . .

MEMORY CHALLENGE

2 Corinthians 9:9

As it is written: "He has scattered abroad his gifts to the poor; his righteousness endures forever."

Jesus himself reached more people preaching on the mountain, but he touched more lives walking down the street, writing in the sand. . . .

Praising God is a good thing. Honoring God is a better thing. . . .[2]

It is true! The best witness for Jesus Christ is not what the believer says but the life he or she lives. God has not called most of us to be preachers, but He has called and gifted every believer to witness to others and to represent Him to those with whom he or she comes in contact. Christians are ministers of Jesus Christ every day and in every way.

A familiar saying is that "actions speak louder than words." You've probably heard it said of certain individuals that "They talk the talk, but they don't walk the walk." Be careful that no careless or undisciplined action be a stumbling block to a weaker brother or sister or be an excuse that could be used by someone to reject Christ.

4. Read 1 Corinthians 8. The lesson that Paul is teaching here goes far beyond just a question of food. Record verse 9.

5. Read Romans 14:12-21, and record verse 13.

What is the kingdom of God? See verse 17.

Why is that so? See verse 18.

Summarize verse 21.

Several Christian men met together often for fellowship and friendly competition. One of their favorite games involved using dice. They invited Brad, who was a brand-new Christian, to join them. With God's help, Brad was fighting a serious addiction to gambling. One form of gambling that he had practiced also involved using dice. His friends quietly and discreetly put away that game after he joined them.

None of the friends felt that using the dice was wrong. But none of them had ever been gamblers. They did not want their fun, innocent for them, to be a "stumbling block" for Brad, who felt conviction over his former use of dice and felt that he should avoid any use of them. Have you ever given up something to keep from being a "stumbling block" to someone else?

6. *Live by the Spirit and you will not gratify the desires of the sinful nature* (Galatians 5:16). The transforming work of the Holy Spirit in the life of the believer produces a life that pleases God. From the following verses, list the actions and attitudes of the sinful nature. Then list the Spirit-led qualities in the life of a Christian that present a positive witness to the world.

Galatians 5:19-23, 26
Sinful nature

Spirit-led life

Ephesians 5:3-5, 8-10
Sinful nature

Spirit-led life

7. Philippians 2:14 adds, *Do everything without complaining and arguing.* Why? Summarize Philippians 2:15-16.

God loved us and chose us in Christ to be holy and without fault in his eyes. . . . Those who claim they belong to the Lord must turn away from all wickedness. So get rid of all malicious behavior and deceit. Don't just pretend to be good! . . . Be careful how you live among your unbelieving neighbors. Even if they accuse you of doing wrong, they will see your honorable behavior, and they will believe and give honor to God when he comes to judge the world (Ephesians 1:4; 2 Timothy 2:19; 1 Peter 2:1, 12, NLT).

DAY TWO

Endurance

Read 2 Corinthians 6:4-5.

1. How did Paul refer to himself and his fellow workers?

Endurance "does not describe the frame of mind that can sit down with folded hands and bowed head and let a torrent of troubles sweep over it in passive resignation. It describes the ability to bear things in such a triumphant way that it transforms them."[1]

2. Paul had already written briefly about his hardships (1:8-9; 4:8-9) and would do so again (11:23-29). In today's passage Paul lists nine conditions of endurance—in three groups of three each.

List those presented in general terms (the first three).

List the next three sufferings inflicted by others.

List the three disciplines that Paul had imposed upon himself in order to further the gospel.

Numerous accounts in Acts give more details. Paul had faced angry mobs in nearly every city, usually being stirred up by the Jews. He was severely beaten several times and imprisoned at least four times—in Philippi, Jerusalem, Caesarea, and Rome. He worked hard; in addition to his teaching and preaching, he earned his own living by working as a tentmaker. He spent sleepless nights and often went without food (2 Corinthians 11:27).

3. Read the words of Jesus to His disciples that are recorded in Luke 21:12-19. According to verse 13, what will be the result of suffering persecutions in His name?

Why did Jesus say that they need not worry about how they would defend themselves?

Record verse 19.

Through the years since Paul's ministry, Christian pastors and teachers have continued to be persecuted for refusing to deny Christ. Just a few weeks before this lesson was written, 52 pastors of Chinese house churches were imprisoned. Christian laypeople, even children, are suffering persecution also.

A pastor was arrested and tortured for his Christian work. His son was beaten by the Muslim guards in order to try to force the father to say what they wanted. The son told his father to withstand and that if they killed him, he would die with the word "Jesus" on his lips. The son was killed.[2]

In Pakistan, Saleema led her Muslim friend, Raheela, to the Lord. For this, Raheela was murdered by her parents, and Saleema was thrown in prison, where she faced unspeakable torture. Today she is studying God's Word and hopes to become a missionary among her own people.[3]

Radical Islamic troops have been waging jihad against the island people of Indonesia. Jihad attacks against Christians claimed as many as 10,000 lives in the three years prior to June 2002. Christians have been robbed, their homes, businesses and churches burned.[4]

An 18-year-old Indonesian, Johannes, was caught by radical Muslims and told to become a Muslim or be killed. Assured of his salvation and prepared to die, Johannes said no. He was struck in the temple with the tip of a samurai sword, and his left shoulder and forearm were slashed. A gaping wound was ripped into the back of his neck, nearly severing his head. His back and legs were slashed. He was covered with banana leaves; they attempted to set them on fire, but the leaves were too green. Johannes was left for dead.

Johannes cried out to God and suddenly felt enough strength to escape. One night, after seeing no one for eight days, he collapsed and cried out to God again. Suddenly he felt a comforting, peaceful, reassuring touch. There was no answer when he called out. The person with the comforting touch had disappeared, but Johannes felt a warm surge of energy and regained enough strength to continue on. He believes that the visitor was Jesus.

Today Johannes is studying to become an evangelist. He believes his life was spared so that he could lead Muslims to Christ.[5]

These persecutions continue in many parts of the world. Christians in the United states today face a different challenge. William Barclay wrote in 1954, "Nowadays it is not the violence but the mockery or amused contempt of the crowd against which the Christian must stand fast."[6] This is even truer today. Christian leaders who have spoken out against evil have been ridiculed for their biblical beliefs and have even received threats of bodily harm.

4. Have you ever received ridicule or discrimination, not because of foolish statements or actions but because of your stand for Christ? Explain.

5. Acts 14:22 says that *we must go through many hardships to enter the kingdom of God*, and 2 Timothy 2:3 tells us to *endure hardship . . . like a good soldier of Christ Jesus*. What makes that possible according to the following verses?

1 Chronicles 16:11

1 Corinthians 16:13

Hebrews 12:1-2

What are the rewards for endurance according to the following verses?

Matthew 24:13

2 Timothy 2:12

James 1:12

Revelation tells us that the overcomers will never have their names blotted from the book of life, will be given the right to sit with Christ on His throne, and will inherit all the blessings of the new heaven and earth as sons and daughters of God (3:5, 21; 21:1-7). *Lord, teach me endurance, and give me the strength to be an overcomer.*

MEMORY CHALLENGE

What has God scattered abroad?

DAY THREE

Weapons of Righteousness

Read 2 Corinthians 6:6-7.

1. In 2 Corinthians 6:4-5 Paul lists nine difficulties he had met with great endurance. In 2 Corinthians 6:6-7 Paul gives nine scriptural characteristics he was able to demonstrate in his life even in the midst of adversity. List these nine spiritual qualities.

These nine characteristics are the goal of every true follower of Christ. It is the presence and power of the Holy Spirit in our lives that makes it possible.

Purity: Paul kept his heart and life free from impure acts or motives. *Do not share in the sins of others. Keep yourselves pure* (1 Timothy 5:22).

Understanding: Paul had knowledge of God's truth and His work in Christ. *Now this is eternal life: that they may know you, the only true God, and Jesus Christ, whom you have sent* (John 17:3).

2. Give two or three examples of how we may receive increased understanding of the things of God.

Patience: Paul endured injuries, insults, stubbornness, and stupidity without anger or revenge.[1] *We urge you . . . be patient with everyone* (1 Thessalonians 5:14).

Kindness: Paul considered the need of others over his own. *Be kind and compassionate to one another, forgiving each other* (Ephesians 4:32).

In the Holy Spirit: In everything Paul did or said, he displayed the presence and power of the Holy Spirit indwelling in his life. *And I will ask the Father, and he will give you . . . the Spirit of truth. . . . He lives with you and will be in you* (John 14:16-17).

In sincere love: Paul displayed genuine love that reflected the attitude of Christ. *Love must be sincere* (Romans 12:9). *Love one another deeply, from the heart* (1 Peter 1:22).

3. Read 1 Corinthians 13:1-13 and personalize a one-sentence summary of this passage.

In truthful speech: Paul had asked for prayer that he might *declare [the gospel] fearlessly, as I should* (Ephesians 6:20). He had preached God's message even when the truth was unpopular. Jesus said, *When he, the spirit of truth, comes, he will guide you into all truth. . . . [The Father's] word is truth. . . . If you hold to my teaching . . . then you will know the truth, and the truth will set you free"* (John 16:13; 17:17; 8:31-32).

In the power of God: Paul always acknowledged that *this all-surpassing power is from God and not from us* (2 Corinthians 4:7). *What is impossible with men is possible with God* (Luke 18:27). *For nothing is impossible with God* (Luke 1:37).

4. Record Ephesians 6:10.

With weapons of righteousness in the right hand and the left: In the Roman Empire, weapons in the right hand were offensive weapons. Weapons in the left hand were considered defensive weapons.

5. Read Ephesians 6:11-18. According to verse 17, what was Paul's offensive weapon of righteousness?

According to verse 13-18, what were his defensive weapons of righteousness?

Though we live in the world, we do not wage war as the world does. The weapons we fight with are not the weapons of the world. On the contrary, they have divine power (2 Corinthians 10:3-4).

MEMORY CHALLENGE

What endures forever?

DAY FOUR

Paradox

Read 2 Corinthians 6:8-10.

A paradox is "a statement seemingly absurd or contradictory, yet in fact true."[1]

1. In this passage Paul makes nine paradoxical statements. The first four contrast how his critics viewed him and his ministry with how God evaluated them. After each opinion that reflected the worldly human view, record how God (and believers who looked on the "unseen") regarded his ministry.

   Dishonor

   Bad report

   Imposters

   Unknown

2. The last five statements name actual physical and emotional conditions that Paul had suffered contrasted with the positive, even victorious, response of a person totally committed to Christ.

   Complete each paradox:

   Dying

   Beaten

   Sorrowful

   Poor

   Having nothing

   A similar pairing of contrasting statements is found in 2 Corinthians 4:7-10.

As was true for Paul, most faithful ministers will probably be honored and approved by most but dishonored and disapproved by some. There are people who attend church regularly but don't really want to be confronted with the truth of God's Word; they want a watered-down, feel-good religion. "Christian leaders are especially vulnerable to criticism from others, pride (if they are successful), depression (if they fail), and Satan's constant efforts to destroy their work for God."[2]

Every faithful minister and teacher needs support, encouragement, love, and prayer from his or her people; this helps to provide him or her with the strength to stand firm and maintain a positive spirit under pressure.

3. How did Paul ask the Ephesians to pray for him? See Ephesians 6:19.

4. Read Hebrews 13:17-18. Why does the writer of Hebrews tell us to obey our leaders (verse 17)?

   What are we asked to do in verse 18?

Do you pray regularly for your pastor, your Sunday School teacher, and your Bible study leaders? Plan to spend at least five minutes daily to pray for your pastor and at least another five minutes for your teachers.

Turn off the radio when you are driving alone, and instead, lift up your Christian leaders in prayer. Even scrubbing floors and mowing lawns can be times spent with the Lord. These are not substitutes for regular set-apart times of prayer, but this kind of prayerful attitude, I believe, is what Paul meant when he said to *pray continually* (1 Thessalonians 5:17).

5. Write a brief note of appreciation and encouragement this week to your pastor and/or teacher.

All Christians could make these statements of paradox as they walk with Christ through troubles and difficulties. We all know, or have known, people who were dying physically yet were radically alive in Christ and in their assurance that they would soon be with Him. We might be very poor in the eyes of the world, but we can share the riches of God in Christ with our friends and neighbors. We might have little in the way of material possessions, but we have God's abundant grace and the presence and power of the Holy Spirit in our lives—and that is of priceless worth.

6. Record Proverbs 28:6.

7. According to James 2:5, what has God chosen [for] those who are poor in the eyes of the world?

In June 2003 two teenaged sisters attended a youth rally in Oklahoma City held in preparation for the upcoming Billy Graham Crusade. Excited to be a part of the planning, they loaded their car with posters and flyers and headed south on the interstate. A passing truck clipped their car; the older girl lost control, and the car flew across the median and into oncoming traffic, where it was hit by two northbound vehicles. The older sister, who was driving, was killed; the younger sister was seriously injured and unconscious.

The girls' Christian parents were interviewed several times by the media. Even through their intense grief, with tears streaming down their faces, they rejoiced publicly in the comfort and love of their Savior in the midst of this tragedy—*sorrowful, yet always rejoicing* (2 Corinthians 6:10). What a powerful witness for Christ!

The ability to withstand adversity and remain faithful and victorious is found in another paradox, these words of Jesus: *Whoever wants to save his life will lose it, but whoever loses his life for me will find it. What good will it be for a man if he gains the whole world, yet forfeits his soul?* (Matthew 16:25-26).

8. What do you think that passage from Matthew means for your life?

To be a true follower of Christ means to have a deep and sincere commitment to His service. Radical obedience may sometimes mean experiencing loneliness, discomfort, pain, or even death. But if we allow our fears and reluctance to cause us to disobey, we may lose God's intended purpose for our lives and begin to die spiritually. We may have purposeful living in the present and eternal life with Christ in heaven in the future only if we give ourselves without reservation to Christ and His call to service.

MEMORY CHALLENGE

Paul said that he had nothing and yet possessed everything (6:10). Explain how that might relate to this week's memory verse.

DAY FIVE

Open Your Hearts

Read 2 Corinthians 6:11-13; 7:2-4.

1. Paul had *spoken freely* to the Corinthians. What else had he done for them?

2. What were the Corinthians withholding from Paul that he had not withheld from them?

3. What did he ask of the Corinthians?

How is a similar thought expressed in 7:2?

4. Continuing in chapter 7, list three things Paul had not done in his ministry to the Corinthians.

5. Record three positive statements that were the reason for his joy knowing no bounds.

Paul reflected on what he had written to the Corinthians and knew that he had spoken from a heart of love for them. He had given them an honest report of the good and the failures in his life. He had grieved over the situation in Corinth and over their lack of confidence in him, but he had not written to grieve them. He wanted to let them know the depth of his love for them (2:3).

The Corinthians were not returning Paul's love. Paul was their spiritual father; he had founded the church at Corinth (1 Corinthians 4:14-15). But under the influence of the false preachers, some of the people were rejecting Paul. Instead of accepting criticism or instruction given to us out of love and concern for our spiritual welfare, we sometimes respond negatively toward our God-called and Christ-led spiritual leaders. "We need an open rather than a closed heart toward God's messengers."[1]

Paul defended himself once again; he had wronged no one, corrupted no one, and exploited no one. He had not exploited the church at Corinth for his own financial gain. Later in this letter he would ask them, *Did I exploit you through any of the men I sent you? . . . Titus did not exploit you, did he? Did we not act in the same spirit and follow the same course?* (2 Corinthians 12:17-18).

6. Summarize 2 Corinthians 11:7-9.

The Greek word translated "corrupted" means "injured" or "destroyed." False prophets and teachers in the church at Corinth were twisting and distorting the teachings of Jesus and the apostles. But Paul's teachings had not injured or destroyed their faith; he spoke before God with sincerity (2:17). *We do not use deception, nor do we distort the word of God*, Paul had told them. *On the contrary*, he had set forth *the truth plainly* (2 Corinthians 4:2).

7. How did Paul refer to these false teachers in 2 Corinthians 11:13?

Record 11:15.

Are there preachers and teachers today who compromise the absolute truth of God's Word? Are we more concerned with people's money than we are with their souls? *God, help us to be faithful!*

Why were some of these Corinthians withholding their affection from Paul? Was it because, as mentioned in 1 Corinthians 5, he had disciplined them for their failure to rebuke sin in their midst? Was it because the false teachers had influenced them with negative criticism of Paul? Or was it an effort to use the withholding of affection as a weapon to try to control Paul and get him to say things their way? Perhaps it was all of these.

Despite the Corinthians' lack of affection, Paul lovingly commended those who had accepted his discipline, remained loyal to him and to his teachings, and were maturing in their faith.

Are you able to accept discipline graciously when it is given from a heart of love and concern? Are you able to respond with love even when someone withholds his or her affection? Ask God to open your heart.

MEMORY CHALLENGE

Record the first two phrases of Psalm 112:9.

"Do Not Be Yoked with Unbelievers"

Read 2 Corinthians 6:14-18.

1. Record 2 Corinthians 6:14.

2. Paul used five rhetorical questions to pair things that have nothing in common. A rhetorical question is one that is primarily for literary effect; the answer is implied in the question. List each pair.

   Example: righteousness—wickedness

   (Note: Belial was a name for Satan.)

3. *We are* _____ _____ _____

   _____ _____ _____ (verse 16).

4. What has God said?

What did Paul mean when he wrote, *Do not be yoked together with unbelievers*? Is a Christian supposed to walk away from an established marriage relationship or business partnership with a nonbeliever? No! Paul made it clear that a Christian was to stay, if possible, with a non-Christian spouse. He had previously written to the Corinthians, *To the married*

I give this command (not I, but the Lord): A wife must not separate from her husband. . . . and a husband must not divorce his wife (1 Corinthians 7:10-11).

5. Summarize Paul's instructions in 1 Corinthians 7:12-13, 15.

Paul was probably referring to God's command in Deuteronomy 22:10: *Do not plow with an ox and a donkey yoked together*. These animals are different in strength and size and cannot pull a plow evenly. In the same way, the believer and nonbeliever basically are so different that a partnership could lead to disaster and weaken, or even destroy, the faith, commitment, and Christian standards of living of the believer. So Paul was urging believers not to form any new long-term, binding relationships with nonbelievers and to get out of any that were harmful to their faith.

However, Paul was not telling believers to isolate themselves from nonbelievers. In fact, he had written, *In that case you would have to leave this world* (1 Corinthians 5:10). "For the sake of winning [people], Paul would seek to conform to the pattern of culture in which he found himself (1 Corinthians 9:19-23)—not, however, at the expense of the integrity of the Christian faith and its moral standards."[1]

Paul was calling them to a radical ethical separation from a worldly, pagan environment. Idolatry and immorality were embedded in the culture of Corinth. Apparently some believers were having difficulty separating themselves from these practices.

Much of the entertainment and socializing in Corinth involved feasts that included toasts to the pagan gods. Many jobs and crafts involved the making of idols or the sewing of garments for the pagan priests. Obedience to Christ would result in some radical changes in the believers' lives. Obedience to Christ might result in some radical changes in your life and mine.

These admonitions from Paul to the church at Corinth are for every church and every believer today. Sometimes it was the church, the Body of Christ, whom Paul referred to as God's temple (1 Corinthians 3:16). At other times Paul referred to the individual believer as the temple of God (1 Corinthians 6:19-20).

Yes, every believer is a *temple of the living God*, where His Holy Spirit dwells. I want to be a temple fit for His presence, don't you? And that involves avoiding any activity or entertainment or fellowship that might damage my influence with others or lead to sin.

> *"So leave the corruption and compromise,*
>   *leave it for good" says God.*
> *"Don't hook up with those who will pollute you.*
>   *I want you all for myself.*
> *I'll be a Father to you;*
>   *you'll be sons and daughters to me."*

—2 Corinthians 6:17-18, TM

MEMORY CHALLENGE

Try to quote 2 Corinthians 9:9 from memory.

2 Corinthians

■ **A Study of 2 Corinthians 7:1—9:5**

DAY ONE

"Perfecting Holiness"

Read 2 Corinthians 7, concentrating on verse 1.

1. What are the *promises* Paul is referring to? Review 2 Corinthians 6:16-18.

2. *Since we have these promises*, what are we to do?

Verse 1 of chapter 7 is the conclusion to the commands and promises found in 6:14-18. Paul had commanded that the Corinthians remove all worldliness from their personal lives and the church (verses 14, 17). We, too, have that command. He had given a reason—*that we are the temple of the living God* (verse 16). And he had also given these promises from God: *I will live with them and walk among them, and I will be their God. . . . I will receive you, I will be a Father to you, and you will be my sons and daughters* (verses 16-18).

Paul summed up this way the commands he had given: *Let us purify ourselves from everything that contaminates body and spirit.* To purify is to free from sin or defilement.

1 Timothy 5:22 says to *keep yourself pure*. Any person or thing that is pure is "free from . . . contact with that which weakens, impairs, or pollutes . . . free from moral defilement."[1]

Paul told us to think about things that are pure, lovely, and praiseworthy (Phil. 4:8). Think about the television programs and movies you have watched or the books you have read recently. Was there anything that could cause you to have impure thoughts that contaminate the body and spirit? Ask God to forgive you. And change your reading and viewing habits!

3. What did Jesus promise in Matthew 5:8?

"Holiness [is] the state or condition of being holy, sanctified, saintly, consecrated. The root idea is that of 'separation' or 'apartness.' . . . Holiness . . . came to mean that kind of separation or apartness which could mark personal character. . . . This more ethical conception of the divine holiness meets us everywhere in the N.T. . . . Holy love involves complete separation from sin, but at the same time profound concern for the sinner and devotion to the task of rescuing him.

MEMORY CHALLENGE

2 Corinthians 9:10

He who supplies seed to the sower and bread for food will also supply and increase your store of seed and will enlarge the harvest of your righteousness.

"Christian holiness is the quality of life and character which comes from being 'in Christ' (2 Corinthians 5:17), from being 'indwelt' by Christ (Galatians 2:20)." It is then that we become *a dwelling in which God lives by his Spirit* (Ephesians 2:22). Yet Paul "never thinks of the holiness or sanctification as being complete; it is always something yet to be perfected (2 Corinthians 13:9; Ephesians 4:12)."[2]

4. What does Paul pray for the believers in 2 Corinthians 13:9?

Adam Clarke calls perfecting holiness "getting the whole mind of Christ brought into the soul." Isn't that a great thought? "This," he says, "is the grand object of a genuine Christian's pursuit."[3]

5. In the Old Testament we find the charge God made to the Israelites to maintain holiness through obedience to the law. What does God command in the following verses?

Leviticus 11:44

Leviticus 20:26

While holiness or "sanctification is a fundamental doctrine of Christianity, and of vast importance to the Church, there are few subjects in theology concerning which there is a greater variety of opinion. All evangelical Christians hold that it is a Bible doctrine, that it includes freedom from sin, that it is accomplished through the merits of Christ's death, and that it is the heritage of those who are already believers. There is much difference, however, as to its exact nature and the time of its attainment."[4]

The purpose of this lesson is not to debate the exact nature of sanctification nor the time it is received by the believer. The purpose here is to show that holiness is the New Testament standard for Christian experience. Just as God commanded the Israelites, it is still His will and command that His people be holy.

6. The New Testament demands holiness. Record 1 Peter 1:15-16.

He chose us in him before the creation of the world to be holy and blameless in his sight (Ephesians 1:4). *You were taught . . . to put off your old self . . . to be made new in the attitude of your minds; and to put on the new self, created to be like God in true righteousness and holiness* (Ephesians 4:22-24).

It is God's will that you should be sanctified. . . . For God did not call us to be impure, but to live a holy life. Therefore, he who rejects this instruction does not reject man but God, who gives you his Holy Spirit (1 Thessalonians 4:3, 7-8). *Therefore, I urge you, brothers, in view of God's mercy, to offer your bodies as living sacrifices, holy and pleasing to God—this is your spiritual act of worship* (Romans 12:1).

It is the presence of the Holy Spirit in our lives that enables us to live our lives in the purity of holiness. We have these promises: *I will put my Spirit in you and move you to follow my decrees and be careful to keep my laws* (Ezekiel 36:27). *Repent and be baptized, every one of you, in the name of Jesus Christ for the forgiveness of your sins. And you will receive the gift of the Holy Spirit* (Acts 2:38). *You will receive power when the Holy Spirit comes on you* (Acts 1:8).

How, then, do we go about the task of perfecting holiness? *Let's make a clean break with everything that defiles or distracts us, both within and without. Let's make our entire lives fit and holy temples for the worship of God* (2 Corinthians 7:1, TM).

Is there anything from which you need to make a clean break? Do you have the presence and power of the Holy Spirit in your life to help you stay pure and undefiled, a fit and holy temple to be a dwelling place for God's Holy Spirit? Ask God to help you grow and mature and become more and more like Christ.

7. If you have made that "clean break" and know that the Holy Spirit indwells your life, what are some things that would help you to grow more and more like Christ—perfecting holiness?

And be confident of this, *that he who began a good work in you will carry it on to completion until the day of Christ Jesus* (Philippians 1:6).

Praise be to the Lord, the God of Israel, because he has come and has redeemed his people . . . to enable us to serve him without fear in holiness and righteousness before him all our days (Luke 1:68, 74-75).

DAY TWO

Godly Sorrow Brings Repentance

Read 2 Corinthians 7:5-13, and review the final section of the last paragraph of "Introduction to 2 Corinthians."

In 7:5 Paul resumes the story that he had left in 2:13 about his travels, his change of plans, his troubles, and the *severe letter* he had written.

1. Summarize 2 Corinthians 2:12-13.

Paul had left an open door for evangelization in Troas because of his concern over Titus. He had sent Titus to Corinth with what has come to be called the "severe letter" (see Introduction) and was concerned about Titus's safety, his acceptance by the Corinthians, and their reaction to his letter. So Paul went to Macedonia to see if he could meet up with Titus there.

2. According to 2 Corinthians 7:6-7, in what two ways was Paul comforted?

To whom did Paul give credit for comforting him?

3. What made Paul's joy *greater than ever*?

4. Why did Paul say he did not regret, and even was happy, that his letter had caused sorrow?

5. Look up a brief definition of repentance, and record it here.

6. *Godly sorrow brings repentance that leads to*

_____ . . . *but worldly sorrow brings*

_____ (verse 10).

What do you think Paul meant by *godly sorrow*?

What do you think he meant by *worldly sorrow*?

Harper's Bible Dictionary says that repentance means "turning to God." In turning to God, however, we must also turn away from that which we have come to realize is displeasing to God. The act is accompanied by sorrow for that which makes the repentance necessary. If there is no sorrow, then there is no repentance.[1]

Christian repentance is not limited to crime or vice or to what are called *acts of the sinful nature* (Galatians 5:19). We must repent not merely of the evil things we do but also for our evil thoughts and purposes.[2] Jesus taught us that even the desire to do evil means one has already committed the act in his or her heart (Mark 7:21-23). 1 John 3:15 says, *Anyone who hates his brother is a murderer.*

Worldly sorrow is merely being sorry for the negative consequences to your life or that you got caught. It does not result in a change of attitude and often results in bitterness and resentment. "Sorrow in itself is not repentance, neither is remorse, nor self-condemnation, nor self-loathing, nor external reformation." Worldly sorrow can lead to rebellion against God. It does not bring repentance, but rather, spiritual death.[3]

Godly sorrow leads to a 180-degree turnaround, a complete change of attitudes, views, feelings, and purposes. It involves not only turning away from sin but also turning to God.

Let's look at an example of each kind of sorrow: Judas betrayed Jesus and was seized with remorse. He returned the betrayal money, said, *I have sinned*, and hanged himself (Matthew 27:3-5). That was worldly sorrow.

Peter denied Jesus three times, a different kind of betrayal. The crowing of a rooster reminded him of Jesus' words *Before the rooster crows, you will disown me three times.* Peter wept bitterly (Matthew 26:69-75). He rejoined the disciples and was fishing with them when Jesus appeared on the shore. Peter jumped into the water and swam toward Him. Jesus asked Peter three times if he loved Him, and three times Peter answered, *Yes, Lord . . . you know that I love you.* Peter repented, he was forgiven, and his life was totally changed (John 21:1-17). *Godly sorrow brings repentance that leads to salvation.*

7. List what was produced in the Corinthians by their godly sorrow and repentance (verse 11).

The "one who did wrong" was probably a false teacher who had spoken against Paul. The Corinthians were truly sorry that they had allowed the troublesome situation to develop rather than dealing with it. Their sorrow had led to repentance, and with earnestness, indignation, and justice, they had cleared up the matter and reaffirmed their love for Paul.

Sometimes it is necessary to take action and rebuke someone in love rather than allow a bad situation to continue. Paul did not enjoy inflicting pain on his spiritual children, but this kind of rebuke, given unwillingly but because it is necessary, is the most effective. If there is someone you need to rebuke, ask God to help you confront the individual in love in such a way as to bring repentance.

Is there any action or attitude in your life for which you feel sorrow? God wants a broken spirit and a broken and repentant heart (Psalm 51:17). Now is the time to repent and turn to God, to determine with His help to make that 180-degree turnaround in your life. *If we confess our sins, he is faithful and just to forgive us our sins and purify us from all unrighteousness* (1 John 1:9).

MEMORY CHALLENGE

Who supplies seed to the sower and bread for food? (2 Corinthians 9:10). Refer to 2 Corinthians 9:8.

DAY THREE

Obedience

Read 2 Corinthians 7:13-16.

1. Paul had boasted about the Corinthians. Had they lived up to Paul's expectations?

2. Why was Titus's affection for the Corinthians *all the greater*?

Titus evidently had been concerned about the kind of reception he would receive in Corinth. He would have been aware of the way in which they had been treating Paul and of the turmoil in the church. And Paul had sent him with a harsh letter of reprimand. How would they respond? Paul had boasted of his confidence in them.

Sometimes as a parent, teacher, boss, or friend, you may need to discipline a child, a student, an employee, or a friend. Paul gives us a beautiful example of the importance of following up the discipline by reaffirming our love and affection for them and our confidence in them and in their response.

Paul was greatly encouraged that Titus had been "refreshed" by the Corinthians' acceptance of him and that Titus's affection for them was greatly increased because of their obedience. Probably not everyone had responded properly, but the church as a whole had.

Paul had written the severe letter to *see if [they] would stand the test and be obedient in everything* (2:9), and now Titus had confirmed that obedience.

God has always demanded obedience. He said to His children in Israel, *What does the LORD your God ask of you but to fear the LORD your God, to walk in all his ways, to love him, to serve the LORD your God with all your heart and with all your soul, and to observe the LORD's commands?* (Deuteronomy 10:12-13).

3. What does Deuteronomy 13:4 tell us?

4. Read Luke 6:46-49. Record verse 46.

In one or two sentences, explain the lesson Jesus was teaching in verses 47-49.

5. Record the words of Jesus in the following verses:

Luke 11:28

John 14:15

John 15:10 (first two phrases)

6. Read 1 John 2:3-6. How do we know that we have come to know Jesus?

What did John call the man who says, *I know him*, but does not do what He commands?

How do we *know we are in him*?

If you love me, you will obey what I command. And I will ask the Father, and he will give you another Counselor to be with you forever—the Spirit of truth (John 14:15-17). God does not abandon us as we struggle to be obedient to His will. He has sent His Holy Spirit (John 14:26; Romans 8:11) to walk with us and dwell within us to help us in our weakness (Romans 8:26) and to strengthen us with His power (Ephesians 3:16) when we are submissive to His will and control.

This is love for God: to obey his commands. And his commands are not burdensome (1 John 5:3).

Fear and *trembling* are combined in this context (meaning awe and respect) in other scriptures; for example, in Jeremiah 5:22 and Philippians 2:12.

"Subsequent events, reflected in chapters 10—13, suggest that either Titus's report or Paul's response to it was prematurely optimistic." This is one of the reasons that some scholars believe that chapters 10—13 are remains of the "severe letter" that was delivered by Titus.[1]

MEMORY CHALLENGE

Fill in the blanks:

He who supplies _____ to the sower and _____ for food will also supply and _____ your _____ of _____.

2 Corinthians 9:10

The Grace of Giving

Read 2 Corinthians 8, concentrating on verses 1-7.

Chapters 8 and 9 of 2 Corinthians deal with the offering that Paul had been collecting from the Gentile churches for the church in Jerusalem and the responsibility of the Corinthians to give generously to complete the offering they had started (8:11). These two chapters are the most complete instructions in the New Testament concerning God's plan for giving.

Vernon McGee writes, "The subject changes from Christian living to Christian giving, which is as vital a part as living." He divides these two chapters as follows:
   1. Example of Christian Giving . . . 8:1-6
   2. Exhortation to Christian Giving . . . 8:7-15
   3. Explanation of Christian Giving . . . 8:16—9:5
   4. Encouragement to Christian Giving . . . 9:6-15[1]

1. According to 2 Corinthians 8:1, what had God given the Macedonian churches?

2. What *welled up* out of their trial, joy, and extreme poverty?

3. According to verse 3, how had the Macedonians given?

4. For what did they plead?

5. In what gifts did the Corinthians excel?

In what else did Paul urge them to excel?

6. Why was Paul collecting an offering? Refer to Acts 11:27-30 and Romans 15:26-27.

7. What do the following verses tell us about sharing with others?

   Romans 12:13

   Hebrews 13:16

   1 John 3:17

Paul was using the Macedonian churches as an example to the Corinthians. He hoped that the Corinthian believes would be encouraged in their giving by the generosity of the Macedonians. (The Macedonian churches were in Philippi, Thessalonica, and Berea.) The believers in these churches had suffered intense persecution (Philippians 1:27-30; 1 Thessalonians 1:6; 2:14-15; 3:4). Paul referred to their poverty as being "extreme." Yet their joy overflowed, *the joy given by the Holy Spirit* (1 Thessalonians 1:6), as a result of their new life in Christ Jesus.

Paul wanted the Corinthian believers to understand that the joy and liberality of the Macedonians as a result of the genuineness of God's grace in their lives. The evidence of God's grace in our hearts is demonstrated by our love and generosity toward others.

8. Record the following:

   Matthew 10:8 (last sentence)

Acts 20:35 (the quoted words of Jesus)

The generous giving of the believers in Macedonia, despite their own poverty, was what we refer to as sacrificial giving. The *amount* we give is not as important as *how* and *why* we give. God wants us to give in the same way as those Macedonian believers—with a spirit of willingness and joy, because of our love and concern for those in need and because of our love and dedication to Christ and His kingdom.

It is only when we give ourselves first to the Lord (verse 5) and then completely trust God to supply our needs (see Matthew 6:28-34) that we can begin to give freely and joyfully. "Not only are material possessions gifts from God, but also the willingness to give is a gift from God. God's free *grace*—his undeserved favor—motivates us to give our time, money, and talents more generously to others."[2]

Some Christians find it difficult to trust God to supply their needs and then to give generously—even when they know that it is the Holy Spirit directing them in how much to give. Sometimes giving according to God's will means giving up something that we want or may even think that we need; that is sacrificial giving.

Ask God to help you to *excel in this grace of giving.*

MEMORY CHALLENGE

He who supplies seed to the sower and bread for food will also supply and increase your store of seed. What else will He do?

"When we invest what God has given us in his work, he will provide even more to give in his service" (*Life Application Bible*).

DAY FIVE

Rich Through Christ

Read 2 Corinthians 8:8-9.

1. Jesus was rich, yet for your sakes _____ _____ _____. Why? (Personalize your answer.)

Paul had presented the Corinthians with a model for giving—the churches in Macedonia. Now he gives them—and us—the ultimate model of giving, the gift of God's grace to us through the earthly life and death of His Son, Jesus Christ. In obedience to the will of His Father, Jesus set aside all of His riches, power, glory, privileges, and rights as God to become human. That is what is meant by the words "poor" and "poverty." Although He was born in lowly circumstances, His earthly family was probably no poorer than many Jewish families of the time. His was not economic poverty, but the self-imposed poverty of God leaving His glory and becoming human and dwelling among us.

2. Record the following verses:

John 1:1 (The *Word* is Jesus Christ.)

John 1:14

3. Read Philippians 2:5-8. What was Jesus' nature?

He *made himself nothing*. What nature did He assume?

Theologians use the word "incarnation" to refer to the coming of Jesus to earth as a human. "Incarnation" comes from a Latin word meaning "to be made flesh"—"the union of divinity with humanity in Christ. He was conceived by the power of the Holy Spirit and was born without sin, of the Virgin Mary. The Son of God became man. . . . In assuming a true human body and proper human nature, he became subject to the limitations of the flesh; but he is at once truly God and truly man, and although he has two distinct natures, he is only one person."[1]

Jesus' human nature suffered hunger, fatigue, rejection, ridicule, persecution, betrayal, pain, and death. It is through the human suffering that Jesus accepted when He set aside His glory that we may become rich. The riches we receive are not those of material wealth but the blessings we enjoy as a result of salvation.

4. Name the blessing seen in each of the following verses.

John 3:16

John 10:10

Romans 8:17

Ephesians 1:13

2 Peter 1:4

Paul expected the Corinthians, out of love for Christ, to respond with a generous gift. Does your love for Christ motivate you to give generously of your time, talents, and money?

Your attitude should be the same that Christ Jesus had. Though he was God, he did not demand and cling to his rights as God. He made himself nothing; he took the humble position of a slave and appeared in human form. And in human form he obediently humbled himself even further by dying a criminal's death on a cross. Because of this, God raised him up to the heights of heaven and gave him a name that is above every other name, so that at the name of Jesus every knee will bow, in heaven and on earth and under the earth, and every tongue will confess that Jesus Christ is Lord, to the glory of God the Father (Philippians 2:5-11, NLT).

MEMORY CHALLENGE

Fill in the blanks:

He who supplies _____ to the _____ and _____ for _____ will also supply and _____ your store of _____ and will _____ the harvest of your _____.

2 Corinthians 9:10

DAY SIX

An Acceptable Gift

Read 2 Corinthians 8:10—9:5.

1. What had the Corinthians done *last year*?

   What was Paul asking them to do *now*?

2. According to the last phrase of verse 11, how were they to give?

3. According to verse 12, what made the gift acceptable?

4. In verse 19, what two reasons did Paul give for *the offering, which we administer*?

   What did he and Titus and the others want to avoid?

5. Why were Titus and the two brothers being sent to Corinth in advance of Paul (9:4-5)?

Paul was urging the Corinthians to complete the collection they had begun (8:10-15; 9:1-5). The turmoil in the Corinthian church and the accusations against the integrity of Paul were probably the reasons that the offering had not been completed. Paul also wrote recommendations for Titus and the two unidentified brothers who were being sent ahead to collect the offering and would accompany Paul to Jerusalem with the money (8:18-24).

Paul did not command the Corinthians to give generously but advised them to for their spiritual good. Verses 8-15 provide several principles for giving: (1) give because of your love for Jesus Christ (8:8-9); (2) try your best to fulfill your pledges (8:11; 9:2, 5); (3) your willingness to give is more important than the amount you give (8:12); (4) give in proportion to what God has given you (8:12); and (5) give from your plenty to those in need, and they will help you if you find yourself in need (8:14).

6. What lesson do you think Jesus was teaching us in Luke 21:1-4?

7. Verse 15 refers to God's provision of manna for the Israelites in their desert wanderings. Read Exodus 16:4-5, 17-26, 31 to reacquaint yourself with the story. What happened when they tried to keep more than they needed?

If we hoard our financial resources, holding tightly to resources beyond our needs while failing to help a fellow-believer who is in need, our money, of course, will not become *full of maggots*. But in a sense it will *[begin] to smell* (Exodus 16:20). "Wealth enjoyed at the expense of those in need soon corrupts like hoarded manna."[1]

8. Personalize 1 John 3:17.

Equality (8:13-14) refers to everyone's basic needs being met, not that everything we possess must be equal. We have an obligation to help our fellow believers in need (Galatians 6:10), but they must be willing to do their part as much as they are able (see 2 Thessalonians 3:10, 12). Giving must be done responsibly—generously, out of our abundance, but not to the extent that our basic needs cannot be met— and willingly, as an act of love. As we learned from Luke 21:1-4, it is not the amount we give but the spirit with which we give that's most important.

MEMORY CHALLENGE

Try to quote 2 Corinthians 9:10 from memory. How might this verse relate to today's lesson?

2 Corinthians

■ A Study of 2 Corinthians 9:5—10:6

DAY ONE

God Loves a Cheerful Giver

Read 2 Corinthians 9:5-11.

1. Paul wants the Corinthians to give a generous gift, but not one given _____.

2. Whoever sows sparingly will also _____ _____.

   Whoever sows generously will also _____

   _____.

   What does Proverbs 11:24-25 tell us about the generous person who gives freely?

3. Proverbs 22:9 says, *A generous man will himself be blessed.* Jesus said, *"It is more blessed to give than to receive"* (Acts 20:35). According to the following verses, what other blessings do we receive by being cheerful and generous givers?

   Deuteronomy 15:7-10

Psalm 112:1, 9 (When God exalts the *horn* of an individual, it means that he confers great power and prosperity.)[1]

Isaiah 58:6-9

4. According to 2 Corinthians 9:7, what should each of us give?

5. Read Acts 11:26-30. According to verse 29, how did the disciples (*Christians*) in Antioch give to their Judean brothers?

MEMORY CHALLENGE

2 Corinthians 9:11

You will be made rich in every way so that you can be generous on every occasion, and through us your generosity will result in thanksgiving to God.

How do Deuteronomy 16:17 and Ezra 2:69 tell us to give?

6. With what attitude does God want us to give?

Being able to give cheerfully is a grace given by God (2 Corinthians 8:1; 9:8, 14). "Grace giving means that we really believe that God is the great giver, and we use our material and spiritual resources accordingly. You simply cannot outgive God!"[2]

I want each of you to take plenty of time to think it over, and make up your own mind what you will give. That will protect you against sob stories and arm-twisting. God loves it when the giver delights in the giving (2 Corinthians 9:7, TM).

7. Paul told the Corinthians that their attitude when they gave was more important than the amount that they gave. Read Matthew 6:1-4. According to verse 2, how did Jesus say that we are *not* to give?

According to verse 4, how did He tell us that we *are* to give?

Record verse 4.

When I was a child, gift pledges were often taken publicly in a church service. One of the laymen always pledged the largest amount at his church, usually far more than anyone else. Years later, long after his death, I learned that this pledge gift was the only money that he gave all year. A number of people in that congregation, unable to make large public pledges but giving faithfully from every paycheck, actually gave more for the year. I cannot be the judge of the man's motives and attitudes; only God knows what is in the heart. But I am glad that public pledging is seldom done anymore.

Rick Warren is the pastor of Saddleback Community Church in Lake Forest, California, a megachurch with about 19,000 worshipers each week. Pastor Warren is the author of *The Purpose-Driven Church*, a book that has made money for him and his church. Then in 2002 he wrote *The Purpose-Driven Life*, which was an instant best-seller; 7 million copies had been sold by September 2003.

The money that was coming in was far more than Pastor Warren and his wife could ever have imagined, so they prayed for guidance on how to handle this sudden affluence. They decided that they would not change their lifestyle. They live in a comfortable but modest home and drive modest cars. Through the grace of God, they have learned to be content (see Philippians 4:12). "Having all you need" means taking care of your basic needs, not piling up a fortune for yourself.

In September 2003, Pastor Warren told his congregation that he was paying back to the church the money that he had been paid in the 23 years of his pastorate. He took himself off the church payroll, directing what would have been his pay and most of the proceeds from the book to a foundation to be used by the church to help people in need. An interesting thing happened: the offerings in the services that week were all more than usual!

8. How would the experience of Pastor Warren relate to 2 Corinthians 9:10?

9. Record 2 Corinthians 9:11 from this week's Memory Challenge.

Paul was not promising material blessings when he told them that they would *be made rich in every way*. Sometimes people do receive material blessings, and it is true that when we are obedient in our giving, we become better stewards of our remaining resources. And when we give an amount that God has laid on our hearts, even though we may wonder how we will accomplish it, God supplies the means. But Paul was emphasizing the spiritual benefits of giving, both to ourselves and to others.

10. Read James 2:14-17, and record verse 17.

Money is not the only gift that God asks us to give to others; He also expects us to give generously of our time and service. Some churches and Christian agencies distribute free food, clothing, and volunteer medical and dental services; most need more volunteer help. A hot casserole lovingly prepared for a grieving family can be a gift of love. Or our gift might be a warm coat given to a child without one, a pair of tennis shoes for a child who wants to play basketball, or an after-school program for working mothers or fathers who can't afford child care.

You will probably think of other ways that you might give of your time and of yourself in service. If your heart is willing, God will open your eyes to the needs of a hurting world. If generous, cheerful giving is a problem for you, ask God for His "giving grace."

Father, You have greatly blessed me. I enjoy many freedoms and privileges that some are not able to enjoy. You have graciously supplied my needs. Help me that I might not seek more and more for myself, but give me a cheerfully willing and generous heart that is sensitive and responsive to the needs of others. In Jesus' name. Amen.

DAY TWO

Thanks Be to God!

Read 2 Corinthians 9:11-15.

1. What would be the result of the Corinthians' generosity?

2. For what will people praise God?

Carrying out this social relief work involves far more than helping meet the bare needs of poor Christians. It also produces abundant and bountiful thanksgivings to God. This relief offering is a prod to live at your very best, showing your gratitude to God by being openly obedient to the plain meaning of the Message of Christ. You show your gratitude through your generous offerings to your needy brothers and sisters, and really toward everyone. Meanwhile, moved by the extravagance of God in your lives, they'll respond by praying for you in passionate intercession for whatever you need. Thank God for this gift, his gift. No language can praise it enough! (2 Corinthians 9:12-15, TM).

Paul assured the Corinthians that their giving would not only supply the needs of the suffering believers in Jerusalem but would also result in an overflowing thanksgiving to God.

3. There had been attempts by some Jews to force the Gentile Christians to conform to Jewish laws and to be circumcised, which they considered to be the test of following those laws. (See Genesis 17:9-14; Acts 15:1, 5.) The account of the council meeting that was to have settled this issue is found in Acts 15:1-29. According to verses 8-9, what did Peter say that God had done for the Gentiles?

Some of the Jewish Christians were still suspicious and uncertain of the Gentile believers. But Paul believed that the generous obedience of the Gentiles would result in many *expressions of thanks* to God and would help to erase the distrust of their Jewish brethren. The Jews would then pray for the Gentile believers, and the Body of Christ would be united and strengthened.

Paul expected that all believers would express thanksgiving to God for His many blessings to them. We are told to *always [give] thanks to God the Father for everything, in the name of our Lord Jesus Christ* (Ephesians 5:20), and to *give thanks in all circumstances, for this is God's will for you in Christ Jesus* (1 Thessalonians 5:18).

4. Record Psalm 136:1. (These same words are found in the first verse of Psalms 106, 107, and 118.)

Some of the things for which we should be thankful are found in Psalm 136:4-9, 25. What are they?

What are some other gifts from God for which you are thankful?

5. What do you think Paul meant by God's *indescribable gift*, as stated in 2 Corinthians 9:15?

Record Romans 6:23.

6. Personalize summaries of the following verses:

John 3:16

Galatians 4:4-7

Ephesians 2:8

Ephesians 2:13

He who did not spare his own Son, but gave him up for us all—how will he not also, along with him, graciously give us all things? (Romans 8:32). *Thanks be to God for his indescribable gift!* (2 Corinthians 9:15).

Have you accepted this indescribable gift of God, Jesus Christ, as your Savior? If not, prayerfully read 1 John 1:9, confess your sins, and commit your life to Him.

MEMORY CHALLENGE

Why will you *be made rich in every way*?

By the Meekness and Gentleness of Christ

Read 2 Corinthians 10, concentrating on verses 1-2.

The tone of 2 Corinthians now changes drastically. In the first nine chapters Paul's language had been mostly diplomatic and loving. His defense of himself and his ministry had been fairly mild, certainly not with the harsh language, sarcasm, strong personal defense, and the reproach that he uses in chapters 10—13.

There are several possible reasons for this change of tone in the letter:

- Paul might have been complimentary first so that the Corinthians would be more open to accept criticism later.
- Chapters 10—13 might have been written some time later than the first part of the letter, after Paul had heard more distressing and troubling news from Corinth.
- The first part of the letter might have been addressed to the majority who sided with Paul and the last four chapters addressed to a very vocal minority who were rejecting Paul's authority, actively opposing him, and corrupting the gospel.
- These next four chapters might be part of the "severe letter" written before 2 Corinthians and assumed by most to have been lost (see Introduction).

1. By what attributes of Christ did Paul make his appeal to the Corinthians?

2. In verses 1 and 2, Paul was apparently responding to the accusations that his opponents in Corinth had made against him—by quoting them. What were these accusations?

Paul's enemies had already accused him of not following through on his promises, of not having letters of recommendation, and of lacking the authority of a true apostle. The accusations that he is responding to now are that he is bold and courageous when writing letters from a distance but timid and weak when with them and that he lived by the standards of the world.

3. In 2 Corinthians 10:11, what was Paul's answer to these accusations?

4. Paul's purpose was not to bring honor to himself but to exalt Christ. Read 1 Corinthians 2:1-5. What reason did Paul give for not preaching only *with wise and persuasive words*?

5. Paul pleads with the false teachers in Corinth and their followers not to make it necessary for him to treat them with boldness when he returns to Corinth. What had Paul asked them in 1 Corinthians 4:21?

Paul didn't order or command obedience but wrote instead, *By the meekness and gentleness of Christ, I appeal to you* and *I beg you.* Paul modeled his life on the earthly life of Jesus; if they rejected him (Paul) for being meek and gentle, they were rejecting Christ himself. Jesus never demanded obedience and respect; He simply asked people to believe in Him.

6. What does Matthew 11:29 say about the personality of Jesus during His earthly ministry?

7. Record the words of Jesus in Matthew 5:5.

What was Paul's advice in Philippians 4:5?

8. What do the following verses tell us about gentleness?

Galatians 5:22-23

Ephesians 4:2

1 Timothy 6:11

What is of great worth in God's sight, according to 1 Peter 3:3-4?

Aristotle defined the Greek word used for "gentleness" as the "correct mean between being too angry and being never angry at all. It is the quality of the [person] whose anger is always so controlled that he's always angry at the right time and never at the wrong time. It describes the [person] who is never angry at any personal wrong he may receive, but who's capable of righteous anger when he sees others wronged."[1]

9. Give an example of a time when Jesus demonstrated "righteous anger."

Can you think of some things that should cause "righteous anger" as an appropriate response from Christians?

The word translated in the *New International Version* as "meekness" is difficult to translate accurately into English from the Greek. The *New Living Translation* and the *New Century Version* use the word "kindness." *The Message*

reads, *the gentle but firm spirit of Christ*. English dictionaries give several synonyms for the word "meek," but not all of them reflect the true meaning of the Greek word. The synonyms include: "patient," "kind," "not inclined to anger or resentment," "submissive," and "gentle."

Do you look for the worldly standards of appearance, great speaking ability, charisma, or self-proclaimed knowledge and special enlightenment in your spiritual leaders? Meekness and gentleness may not be particularly admired by worldly standards, but they are attributes of Jesus and beautiful to God.

Take a moment now to thank God for His godly servants, Christlike examples who are totally committed and fully submitted to Christ, the ones who teach *not with wise and persuasive words, but with a demonstration of the Spirit's power, so that your faith might not rest on men's wisdom, but on God's power* (1 Corinthians 2:4-5). And then look for an opportunity to thank them for their faithfulness; they need your words of encouragement.

MEMORY CHALLENGE

What will be the result of your generosity to others?

DAY FOUR

Weapons of Divine Power

Read 2 Corinthians 10:3-5.

1. Paul had to live in his world. Believers today must also live in the world. What do we do differently than what the world does?

Paul's enemies accused him of living by the standards of the world, but he defended himself. Although he lived in the world and had the limitations of being human, his conduct and the weapons he used came from God. Paul was well educated but did not rely on his human knowledge and wisdom, nor did he manipulate people through eloquent speech or deception. His message and methods and his confidence were rooted in the power of God.

2. The weapons of divine power that Paul used are available to all believers. What are these weapons able to demolish?

3. Review Ephesians 6:10-20. Against what is our struggle?

This passage lists a number of weapons of divine power. Beside each piece of armor, record the spiritual weapon it represents:

Belt _____

Breastplate _____

Footwear _____

Shield _____

Helmet _____

Sword _____

And on all occasions _____

4. According to 1 Corinthians 2:12-13, what empowers us to use these weapons to demolish strongholds?

5. What are the strongholds that God's power is able to demolish (2 Corinthians 10:5)?

6. Match the following "strongholds" with the correct verse among those found below.

   Example:
   • Wisdom according to the standards of this age (1 Corinthians 3:18-19)

   • Preaching a different Jesus (_____)

   • Boasting of wisdom (_____)

   • Hollow and deceptive philosophies based on human tradition (_____)

   • Peddling the Word for profit (_____)
   • Using deception and distortion of God's Word

      (_____)

   • Puffed-up knowledge (_____)
   • Rejecting God's Word or handling it falsely

      (_____)
   • Godless chatter and false knowledge (_____)

   Jeremiah 8:8-9
   1 Corinthians 3:18-19
   2 Corinthians 2:17
   2 Corinthians 11:4
   1 Timothy 6:20-21
   Jeremiah 9:23
   1 Corinthians 8:1-2
   2 Corinthians 4:2
   Colossians 2:8

7. Read 1 Corinthians 1:17-31. Record verse 19.

According to verse 20, what has God made foolish?

The foolishness of God is _____ _____

_____ _____.

The weakness of God is _____ _____

_____ _____ (verse 25).

Keep your weapons of divine power up to date and ready to defend and protect yourself and those you love. *Watch out for people who try to dazzle you with big words and intellectual double-talk. They want to drag you off into endless arguments that never amount to anything. They spread their ideas through the empty traditions of human beings and the empty superstitions of spirit beings. But that's not the way of Christ* (Colossians 2:8, TM).

MEMORY CHALLENGE

Write this week's memory verse on a 3" x 5" card, and tape it onto your bathroom mirror or in a place where you'll see it often. Read it aloud each time you see it.

DAY FIVE

Obedient Thoughts

Read 2 Corinthians 10:5-6.

1. What are we to do with every thought?

The arguments and pretensions that Paul was addressing were the thoughts and ideas that prideful human reasoning had brought against the knowledge and truths of God. The Judaizers and other false teachers in Corinth had exalted their human thoughts above God's revealed truths. But God's truths had been revealed to believers through the life and words of Jesus Christ, the inspiration of the Holy Spirit, and the divinely inspired Word of God.

2. The wisdom of God and the wisdom of the world often come into conflict; God's wisdom appears as foolishness to the world (1 Corinthians 1:23). What did Paul say about the foolishness of God in 1 Corinthians 1:25?

Do not deceive yourselves. If any one of you thinks he is wise by the standards of this age, he should become a "fool" so that he may become wise. For the wisdom of this world is foolishness in God's sight. . . . "The Lord knows that the thoughts of the wise are futile" (1 Corinthians 3:18-20).

Clever arguments and attractive and/or dynamic personalities are sometimes used for distortions, corruptions, and watered-down versions of the Word of God. "A rationalist Christian, a philosophizing theologian . . . lays aside the divine for the human, God's wisdom for human wisdom, the infinite and infallible for the finite and fallible."[1] But these stern words are what we learn from 1 Timothy 6:3-4: *If anyone teaches false doctrine and does not agree to the sound instruction of our Lord Jesus Christ and to godly teaching, he is conceited and understands nothing.*

3. How important is it for believers to have a good knowledge and understanding of God's Word? Why?

When the Sadducees questioned Jesus in a failed effort to trap Him, Jesus told them, *You are in error because you do not know the Scriptures or the power of God* (Matthew 22:29). There are those today who either *do not know the Scriptures* or deny their truths because they fail to understand or accept *the power of God.*

4. What do the following scriptures tell us about God's Word?

Psalm 12:6

Psalm 33:4

Romans 15:4

2 Timothy 3:16-17

Hebrews 4:12

1 Peter 1:25

We believers cannot win the battle for our minds using worldly weapons—our own human resources and arguments. Only the weapons of God—truth, righteousness, faith, salvation, the Word of God, prayer, and love (Ephesians 6:14-18; 1 Thessalonians 5:8)—are able to demolish the strongholds erected by human reasoning and pretension. "The success of the Gospel depends on its being presented not as our word, but as God's Word; not as something to be proved, but as something to be believed."[2] The true proclamation of God's Word, *our gospel . . . not simply with words, but also*

with power, with the Holy Spirit and with deep conviction (1 Thessalonians 1:5), has the power to destroy false arguments.

Our human reason and thought must be obedient and submissive to Christ. A familiar saying is that you can't keep birds from flying overhead, but you can keep them from building a nest in your hair. We may not be able to keep from hearing teachings and thoughts based on human reasoning against the Word of God, but we can *take captive every thought to make it obedient to Christ* (1 Corinthians 10:5).

We use our powerful God-tools for smashing warped philosophies, tearing down barriers erected against the truth of God, fitting every loose thought and emotion and impulse into the structure of life shaped by Christ. Our tools are ready at hand for clearing the ground of every obstruction and building lives of obedience into maturity (2 Corinthians 10:5-6, TM).

Close your study today with this prayer: *Lord, give me a spirit of discernment to keep my thoughts focused on and obedient to Your truths.*

MEMORY CHALLENGE

Fill in the blanks:

You will be made _____ in _____ way so that you can be _____ on every _____, and through us your _____ will result in _____ to God.

2 Corinthians 9:11

God's Truth

Read 2 Corinthians 10:1-6.

Paul uses the word "strongholds" to refer to any teaching or belief that would prevent us "from knowing the truth about God and worshipping him."[1] The stronghold in Corinth that concerned Paul was intellectualism, which is not the same as intelligence. Intelligence is a gift from God, and when it is obedient to Christ, it is a powerful witness for Him. Intellectualism is "a pride of intelligence that exalts itself . . . the high-minded attitude that makes people think they know more than they really do,"[2] the belief that they are able to "understand" what God really meant, even if it means distorting or removing portions of God's Word that don't fit their theories.

Who has understood the mind of the LORD? (Isaiah 40:13; Romans 11:34). Record Isaiah 55:8-9.

What is God's truth?

How blessed is God! And what a blessing he is! He's the Father of our Master, Jesus Christ, and takes us to the high places of blessing in him. Long before he laid down earth's foundations, he had us in mind, had settled on us as the focus of his love, to be made whole and holy by his love. Long, long ago he decided to adopt us into his family through Jesus Christ. . . .
Because of the sacrifice of the Messiah, his blood poured out on the altar of the Cross, we're a free people—free of penalties and punishments chalked up by all our misdeeds. And not just barely free, either. Abundantly free! He thought of everything, provided everything we could possibly need, letting us in on the plans he took such delight in making. He set it all out before us in Christ, a long-range plan in which everything would be brought together and summed up in him. . . . It's in Christ that we find out who we are and what we are living for. Long before we first heard of Christ . . . he had his eye on us, had designs on us for glorious living, part of the overall purpose he is working out in everything and everyone (Ephesians 1:3-5, 7-12, TM).

Write 2 Corinthians 9:11 from memory.

2 Corinthians

■ A Study of 2 Corinthians 10:7—11:6

Looking Only on the Surface

Read 2 Corinthians 10, concentrating on verses 7-11.

1. Paul told the Corinthians that in their judgments of him, they were *looking only on the surface of things*. Compare the similarities of 2 Corinthians 10:1 with 10:10.

   (10:1) *timid* when face-to-face
   (10:10)

   (10:1) *bold* when away
   (10:10)

The false teachers had interpreted Paul's love for the Corinthians and his gentleness as signs of weakness and powerlessness. They claimed that Paul had no authority and urged the Corinthians to ignore him. Their judgment of Paul was based on his unimpressive appearance and speaking ability.

This is how Paul was described in a book written about A.D. 200, *The Acts of Paul and Thecla*:

> A man of little stature, thin-haired upon the head, crooked in the legs, of good state of body, with eyebrows meeting, and with nose somewhat hooked, full of grace, for sometimes he appeared like a man and sometimes had the face of an angel.[1]

Paul's physical appearance doesn't sound too impressive, does it? Whether or not this was an accurate description of Paul, some of the Corinthians had been influenced to believe that Paul could not be a true apostle, and they had become blinded to the simplicity of the gospel. Paul wanted the message of salvation through Christ to speak for itself and not to be dependent on human speaking ability or philosophy.

2. Summarize how Paul described his preaching in 1 Corinthians 2:1-2.

The false teachers boasted of their *letters of recommendation* (2 Corinthians 3:1), but Paul's authority came from the Lord (Acts 9:15; 2 Corinthians 5:18-20). His ministry to the Corinthians was proven: Their lives had been changed

2 Corinthians 9:12

This service that you perform is not only supplying the needs of God's people but is also overflowing in many expressions of thanks to God.

(2 Corinthians 3:3); he was faithful in presenting the gospel (4:1-5); he had conducted himself in holiness and sincerity (1:12); and he had endured hardships for the cause of Christ (6:3-10; 11:23-28).

God often uses people who appear weak or insignificant by worldly standards to fulfill His purposes. *The LORD does not look at the things man looks at. Man looks at the outward appearance, but the LORD looks at the heart* (1 Samuel 16:7). When God needs an obedient servant, He does not look *only on the surface*.

3. God called Moses to deliver His people out of their bondage to Pharaoh and the Egyptians (Exodus 3:1—4:17). What reason did Moses give for being inadequate to carry out the assignment (4:10)?

What was the Lord's reply (4:11-12)?

4. According to Jeremiah 1:6, what excuse did Jeremiah use when the Lord called him to be His prophet?

According to Jeremiah 1:7-9, what was the Lord's reply?

God uses obedient people from all backgrounds and walks of life. Gideon was a farmer, called to save Israel from her enemies (Judges 6:11-16). David was a shepherd boy, chosen to be Israel's king (1 Samuel 16:1, 6-13). Amos was a shepherd, chosen to be a prophet (Amos 7:14-15). Peter and Andrew were fishermen, chosen to be Jesus' disciples (Matthew 4:18-19). Matthew was a tax collector, chosen to be a disciple (Matthew 9:9).

Twice in recent years my church has been privileged to have David Ring as a guest speaker. David has cerebral palsy, which makes speaking difficult for him. *Looking only on the surface*, we might assume that God could not use him very effectively in ministry. But He has. Many have come to know the Lord through the ministry of this obedient servant of Christ.

One of the most interesting and persuasive preachers that I have heard about was "Uncle Buddy" Robinson. Bud Robinson was a poor, wild, young Texas cowboy before he was saved in a camp meeting and called to preach in 1880. He learned to read and write for the first time from a copy of the New Testament given to him after his conversion.[2] He lisped and was told that "he stuttered so badly and had so little sense, [he] would bring reproach on the church and do more harm than good."[3]

Everyone with whom he talked "was sure that God would not call one like him to preach the gospel."[4] Yet Bud Robinson became a camp meeting favorite as a preacher and has been quoted frequently by other preachers.[5] "It has been said that at one time he knew and could quote from memory at least one-fifth of the Bible."[6] He once estimated that he had "preached 33,000 times and that he saw 100,000 people seek the Lord in the meetings where he preached."[7]

Most of us will not be called, as Paul was, to go to a foreign country or to preach the gospel. Some callings will require study, training, or more education; others will require mostly obedience and a willing spirit. Perhaps God has asked you to teach a Sunday School class or lead a Bible study group, and you have felt inadequate or intimidated. Has God ever asked you to share Christ with a neighbor or friend, but you hesitated because you did not feel that you would make a good impression?

Paul *became a servant of this gospel by the gift of God's grace given [to him] through the working of [God's] power* (Ephesians 3:7). And Paul said that he could *do everything through him who gives me strength* (Philippians 4:13). God will do this for you!

5. God has given us many promises of His strength, wisdom, and power that we may enjoy if we obediently respond to His call. A few are listed below. Personalize the following verses.

Isaiah 41:10

Luke 1:37

2 Corinthians 12:9

Ephesians 3:20

What is God calling you to do for Him? When He calls you to a task, don't look *only on the surface of things*. Be obedient, and trust God to lead you and give you guidance and direction. Trust Him for His power and strength to carry out the task He has assigned to you. *For God did not give us a spirit of timidity, but a spirit of power, of love and of self-discipline* (2 Timothy 1:7). Where we see only the impossibilities, God sees great possibilities!

Building Up or Pulling Down?

Read 2 Corinthians 10:7-11 again, concentrating on verse 8.

1. For what did Paul say that the Lord had given him authority?

"The difference between Paul and the Judaizers was this: Paul used his authority to build up the church, while the Judaizers used the church to build up their authority."[1] Replace the words "the Judaizers" with "some church members," and that statement could be just as true today. Paul's letters are as relevant and meaningful to us as they were to the early churches. We, too, can use our gifts to build up our church, or we can build up ourselves by words and actions that pull down the church.

2. What is the Church, according to the following verses?

Romans 12:5

Ephesians 2:19-22

God has given every believer the "authority" to build up the Body of Christ—the Church. When we make personal attacks on each other or on the policies and plans made prayerfully by our leaders, we destroy the unity of our church fellowship and damage our witness to the watching world. And God is not pleased! In fact, Paul told the church at Corinth that they were *still worldly . . . since there is jealousy and quarreling among you* (1 Corinthians 3:3).

3. Record 1 Corinthians 1:10.

4. How may we build up each other in the church according to the following verses?

Romans 12:10, 15-16, 18

Colossians 3:12-15

"Building up" instead of "pulling down" one another is important, not only in the church but in all our relationships—with our family members, with our friends, and with all others with whom we come into contact. Harsh or thoughtless words can do immeasurable damage to a marriage or to the healthy self-esteem of children, and friendships can be destroyed. Are your words to others "building up," or are they "pulling down"?

I was shopping in a large discount store when I was startled by a loud crash and the sound of a woman screaming at a small child, "You stupid, clumsy idiot—you never do anything right!" A boy, perhaps three or four years old, had bumped into a display in the aisle, sending several boxes crashing to the floor.

Perhaps that mother was tired and stressed, but even if something had been damaged, no one deserves that kind of verbal abuse. Nothing was broken, however, and no irreparable harm was done to the display. But the child's heart, I'm sure, was broken and his spirit crushed. "You stupid, clumsy idiot—you never do anything right!" Is that how that little boy will always see himself? My heart ached for him.

5. From Proverbs 10 (verses 11, 31-32) we learn that *the mouth of the righteous is a fountain of life and brings forth wisdom, and the lips of the righteous know what is fitting.* What do the following verses in Proverbs 15 tell us about "building up" and "pulling down" with words?

Verse 1

Verse 4

6. Record Ephesians 4:29.

We do see praise a bit overdone sometimes. Too much undeserved praise can give a child a distorted view of himself or herself. Proverbs 28:23 says that *serious reprimand is appreciated far more than bootlicking flattery* (TM). But *serious reprimand* means "building up" character with constructive, helpful instruction and discipline, not "pulling down" self-esteem with destructive criticism. Our children, spouses, and other family and friends need to be given praise when it is deserved and when their actions are praiseworthy.

Jesus said, *I tell you that men will have to give account on the day of judgment for every careless word they have spoken* (Matthew 12:36). James 1:26 tells us, *If anyone considers himself religious and yet does not keep a tight rein on his tongue, he deceives himself and his religion is worthless.*

Father, forgive me for the careless words that I have spoken, and "set a guard over my mouth, O LORD; keep watch over the door of my lips" (Psalm 141:3).

> *Lord, make me an instrument of Thy peace:*
> *Where there is hatred, let me sow love;*
> *Where there is injury, pardon;*
> *Where there is doubt, faith;*
> *Where there is despair, hope;*
> *Where there is darkness, light;*
> *Where there is sadness, joy.*
>
> *O Divine Master, grant that I may not so much seek*
> *To be consoled as to console,*
> *To be understood as to understand,*
> *To be loved as to love;*
> *For it is in giving that we receive;*
> *It is in pardoning that we are pardoned;*
> *It is in dying that we are born to eternal life!*
> — Francis of Assisi

MEMORY CHALLENGE

This service that you perform is . . . supplying what?

DAY THREE

Boast in the Lord

Read 2 Corinthians 10:12-18.

1. What did Paul say about people who measure and compare themselves by themselves?

2. To what did Paul say that he would confine his boasting?

3. According to verse 15, what was Paul's hope?

According to verse 16, for what reason?

4. *Let him who boasts boast in* _____ _____ (verse 17).

Why would Paul have felt it necessary to write so much about boasting? The words "boast" and "boasting" are found 20 times in chapters 10, 11, and 12 of 2 Corinthians (NIV). Some of the Corinthians had been impressed and influenced by the false teachers, the Judaizers, who had gone to Corinth "blowing their own horns" and attacking Paul. "There are always those who fall for the arrogant, the bigoted, and the dogmatic."[1]

These false teachers were trying to prove their authority and their greatness as leaders by measuring and comparing themselves by themselves. You've probably heard the expression "They were legends in their own minds." That's a good description of those false teachers! And they could be called a "mutual admiration society." If you weren't a part of their little club, you were nothing. And that's how they considered Paul—nothing, an unimpressive weakling!

The faith of the Corinthians was in danger, and their spiritual growth into maturity in Christ was being compromised. Drastic measures were called for, and Paul used sarcasm, satire, and irony to get his point across.

5. *It is not the one who commends himself who is approved.* Who *is* approved?

Read Ephesians 4:12-16. We are to *become mature, attaining to the whole measure of the fullness of Christ. Then we will no longer be infants.* What can happen to spiritual infants?

Instead, speaking the truth in love, we will do what?

If we compare ourselves with others, we may feel superior or more Christlike. But how do we compare to Christ? How does Christ see us? That is all that really matters! Or we may feel instead that we are a failure compared to what someone else has accomplished. But Paul made it clear to the Corinthians, and to us, that God gives each of us specific gifts and specific areas of service. If we are using our gifts where God has assigned us, God measures us by our obedience and faithfulness, not by what is visibly accomplished or by how we measure up to someone else. There are many different gifts, and every gift, regardless of how unimportant it may seem to us, is necessary for the spiritual life and growth of the church (1 Corinthians 12).

- Are you where God wants you?
- Are you doing the task He has assigned you?
- Are you using for Him the gifts He has given you?

God had given Paul an assignment—to preach the news of Jesus Christ to the Gentiles (Acts 9:15; Romans 15:15-16), and that assignment had been confirmed by the apostles in Jerusalem (Galatians 2:7, 9). Paul was called to be not a pastor but a missionary, to win the Gentiles to Christ and establish churches with the new believers.

6. Record Paul's words in Romans 15:20.

Paul had been the first to arrive in Corinth to preach the gospel (1 Corinthians 3:6), he had laid the foundation (3:10), and he was their father through the gospel (4:15). Now the false teachers were trying to usurp Paul's authority, claiming the Corinthian believers for themselves and turning them against Paul. Their influence had caused dissension and had prevented true spiritual growth in the church. The Corinthians' spiritual immaturity was requiring Paul to take time away from evangelism to other areas in order to try to stabilize the church in Corinth. If the Corinthians would be obedient and grow up into Christ, not only would it free Paul, but they could be a help to him as he carried the gospel to the regions beyond them.

7. *As the Scriptures say, "The person who wishes to boast should boast only of what the Lord has done"* (1 Corinthians 1:31; 2 Corinthians 10:17, NLT).

Complete *what the LORD says* in Jeremiah 9:23-24:

Let not the _____ _____ *boast of*

his _____ *or the* _____ _____ *boast*

of his _____ *or the* _____ _____

boast of his _____*, but let him who boasts boast about this:*

_____ _____ _____

_____ _____ _____, _____

_____ _____ _____ _____.

When we are successful in carrying out an assignment that God has given us, we need to be careful not to commend ourselves or seek praise from others. The praise and glory belong not to us but to God, who gifted us, enabled us, strengthened us, and gave us wisdom for the task. *What you say about yourself means nothing in God's work. It's what God says about you that makes the difference* (2 Corinthians 10:18, TM).

MEMORY CHALLENGE

This service that you perform is overflowing in what?

DAY FOUR

A Pure Virgin to Christ

Read 2 Corinthians 11:1-2.

1. For what reason did Paul say, *I am jealous for you with a godly jealousy (anxious for you with the deep concern of God himself*, TLB)?

The false teachers in Corinth had caused so much turmoil in the church that Paul felt it necessary to silence their accusations. He wanted the church's love to be for Christ alone. That pure devotion was being threatened, so he asked the Corinthians to put up with what he called *foolishness*—boasting of himself. Paul was embarrassed at the necessity of presenting his credentials as an apostle.

Paul's boasting (chapters 11—12) was not empty; it was based on truth. "The apostle puts on a mask to play the role of his opponents. . . . The contradiction between the mask of his boasting and what he is really saying gives this whole passage a unique literary charm and captivating force."[1]

Paul's jealousy for them is the jealousy that God has for His people (Exodus 20:5), a desire for us to give Him all our devotion and faithfulness. "Righteous jealousy is an overwhelming desire for another's well-being, based on sincere love, not self-gratification. Jealousy is portrayed in the Old Testament when God refuses to let his rebellious people self-destruct."[2]

2. Record the first of the Ten Commandments (Exodus 20:3).

God was often pictured in the Old Testament as the Bridegroom of Israel and expressed deep displeasure when His people transferred their love to an object. Paul used the metaphor of marriage to depict Jesus as the Bridegroom of the Church (Ephesians 5:22-32), and Jesus compared himself to a bridegroom (Mark 2:18-20).

In Paul's day, Jewish marriages involved two separate ceremonies, the betrothal and the wedding, usually about a year apart. During that period the girl was regarded legally as the man's wife, but she remained a virgin. . . . Unfaithfulness of a betrothed girl was regarded as adultery and punished as such.[3] The father of the bride had the responsibility of watching over her conduct and presenting her pure to the bridegroom.

Paul was the "father" of the church at Corinth (1 Corinthians 4:15). These converts were promised—"betrothed"—to Christ, and Paul considered it his responsibility to present the church *without stain or wrinkle or any other blemish, but holy and blameless* (Ephesians 5:27) to Christ when He returns to take His bride. We who are believers are the Church. For the Church to be pure and spotless, we must keep our lives pure and holy and love God with all our hearts, souls, and minds (Matthew 22:37).

3. Paul instructed Timothy, *Keep yourself pure* (1 Timothy 5:22). How are the pure blessed, according to Matthew 5:8?

4. *Who may ascend the hill of the LORD and stand in his holy place*, according to Psalm 24:3-4?

Jesus told a parable in which the kingdom of heaven was likened to 10 virgins who went to meet the bridegroom (Matthew 25:1-13). Five virgins were foolish and were not ready and waiting when he came. The five who were ready went in with him to the wedding banquet. The five foolish virgins came later and asked to be let in; the bridegroom told them that he didn't know them.

Let us rejoice and be glad and give him glory! For the wedding of the Lamb has come, and his bride has made herself ready (Revelation 19:7).

I want to be ready when He comes and among the *blessed . . . who are invited to the wedding supper of the Lamb!* (Revelation 19:9). To be invited, our actions, words, thoughts, love, and devotion to God must be kept pure and uncompromised.

MEMORY CHALLENGE

Read 2 Corinthians 9:12 aloud several times. Thank God for supplying *your* needs.

Don't Be Deceived!

Read 2 Corinthians 11:3 and Genesis 3.

1. Paul wanted to present the Corinthian church to Christ as a *pure virgin*. Of what was he afraid?

God commanded Adam to *not eat from the tree of knowledge of good and evil* (Genesis 2:17). Read Genesis 3. Disguised as a serpent, Satan tempted Eve to try the forbidden fruit by questioning God's Word (verse 1) and by implying that God was untruthful and didn't want to share His knowledge (verses 4-5). Seeing that the fruit was good to eat and *desirable for gaining wisdom*, Eve ate some and gave some to Adam.

2. God asked Eve, *What is this you have done?* (verse 13). What was Eve's reply?

Paul realized that the Corinthians faced the same danger, being deceived by Satan into allowing the false teachings to influence them away from their *sincere and pure devotion to Christ*. Satan was seducing them, as he did with Eve, by questioning God's Word, denying it, and substituting his own lies through the teachings of the false prophets.

3. Read Galatians 1:6-12. According to verses 11-12, what did Paul say about the gospel he preached?

The minds of believers are favorite targets for attacks from Satan, and he uses the same tactics to deceive us now as he did with Eve. False teachers can cause us to question God's Word, deny its infallibility, and substitute lies for God's truth. Clever arguments can create doubt and confusion if we allow our thoughts and feelings to be seduced away from our devotion to Christ.

4. Summarize Romans 16:17-18.

The Corinthian believers were impressed and swayed by messages that sounded sensible and good and were skillfully presented. Many of today's false teachings may sound good on the surface. The teacher may be attractive and live a disciplined and moral life, may sound knowledgeable, and often will claim that his or her teachings are from God.

Search the Bible and check every teaching against God's Word, even if it sounds good and seems to make sense. If it contradicts the Word of God, the teaching is false. "We must guard against any teaching that causes believers to dilute or reject any aspect of their faith. Such teaching can be very direct or extremely subtle."[1]

5. What do the following verses say about God's Word?

Psalm 33:4

Proverbs 30:5-6

Isaiah 40:8

Romans 15:4

2 Timothy 3:16

Hebrews 4:12

6. When we read and meditate on God's Word, we need to ask the Holy Spirit to give us wisdom and discernment. What does 1 Corinthians 2:10-11 tell us about the Spirit?

A current belief that all knowledge comes from reasoning is called "intellectualism" or "rationalism." But knowledge of the things of God must not come from reasoning alone but from faith in God, in His power, and in His Word (see Matthew 22:29).

The time will come when men will not put up with sound doctrine. Instead, to suit their own desires, they will gather around them a great number of teachers to say what their itching ears want to hear" (2 Timothy 4:3). *The Lord knows that the thoughts of the wise are futile* (1 Corinthians 3:20).

If anyone teaches false doctrines and does not agree to the sound instruction of our Lord Jesus Christ and to godly teaching, he is conceited and understands nothing (1 Timothy 6:3-4). *See to it that no one takes you captive*

through hollow and deceptive philosophy, which depends on human tradition and the basic principles of this world rather than on Christ (Colossians 2:8).

Father God, protect my mind from anything false. May Your Holy Spirit guide my every thought as I read and study Your Word. In Christ's name I pray. Amen.

MEMORY CHALLENGE

Fill in the blanks:

This service that you _____ is not only _____ the needs of God's _____ but is also _____ in many _____ of _____ to God.

2 Corinthians 9:12

DAY SIX

Preaching Another Jesus

Read 2 Corinthians 11:4-6.

1. In verse 4, what did Paul accuse the Corinthians of putting up with *easily enough*?

Paul was probably not trained in the Greek schools of oratory, but knew what he was talking about. The false teachers were distorting the truth by preaching another Jesus, a spirit other than the Holy Spirit, and a gospel other than God's plan of salvation.

2. Paul believed that the gospel should be simple and understandable. Read 1 Corinthians 2:1-10; summarize verses 1-5.

   According to verse 10, how was God's wisdom revealed to Paul?

The false teachers were probably preaching a gospel based on a worldly view by presenting Jesus only as a powerful miracle-worker and denying the weakness, humiliation, and suffering of the Crucifixion and the power of the Resurrection.

3. According to 1 Corinthians 1:23, what did Paul preach?

4. The false teachers did not preach a gospel that required the self-denial of the Cross. Record the words of Jesus in Mark 8:34.

5. Our *attitude should be the same as that of Christ Jesus* (Philippians 2:5). Briefly explain that kind of attitude (verses 6-8).

And this is the power of the Resurrection for believers: *He who raised Christ from the dead will also give life to your mortal bodies through his Spirit, who lives in you* (Romans 8:11).

MEMORY CHALLENGE

Be prepared to say 2 Corinthians 9:12 from memory with your group.

2 Corinthians

■ A Study of 2 Corinthians 11

DAY ONE

Supplying What Is Needed

Read 2 Corinthians 11, concentrating on verses 7-12.

1. Did Paul receive financial support from the church at Corinth while he was there?

According to verses 7-9, who supported him and supplied his needs?

Paul had just told the Corinthians, *Let him who boasts boast in the Lord* (10:17), but the false teachers had convinced some of the Corinthians believers that Paul was neither an apostle nor qualified to preach. Paul was so concerned about the danger to the faith of these people who had been converted under his ministry that he felt it was necessary to boast of his credentials.

In first-century Greek culture, teachers were able to make a great deal of money; refusing pay was seen as admitting that one's teaching had little value. It was beneath the dignity of Greek professionals to do any kind of work with their hands. "It was more honorable for a traveling teacher to beg than it was for him to stoop to demeaning manual labor."[1] The false teachers considered Paul to be unprofessional and had convinced some of the Corinthian believers that he could be neither competent nor an authority.

2. The Jews, however, respected manual labor. "Jewish rabbis, teachers of the law, were required to support themselves with some kind of trade,"[2] and Paul had been trained in Jewish law and religion. What was Paul's trade (Acts 18:1-4)?

3. Read 1 Corinthians 9:4-14. Did Paul believe that it was wrong for a preacher of the gospel to receive pay? Record what *the Lord has commanded*.

Why, then, did Paul refuse payment from the church in Corinth? There probably were several reasons: (1) He believed that the false teachers were exploiting the Corinthians for financial gain (2 Corinthians 2:17). He did not want these new Christians to think that his preaching was for material gain, and, as a result, possibly miss the message. (2) He may have been accused of improperly using the money being collected for Jerusalem (2 Corinthians 8:20-23; 12:17-18). (3) Perhaps he didn't want to become financially obligated to the Corinthians in order to be able to faithfully preach the gospel free of any undue influence.

The reason Paul gave them, however, was that he needed to *cut the ground from under* the false prophets. Any advantage that he had over them would be gone if their criticism caused him to accept pay. *I'd die before taking your money,* Paul said. *I'm giving nobody grounds for lumping me in*

MEMORY CHALLENGE

2 Corinthians 9:13

Because of the service by which you have proved yourselves, men will praise God for the obedience that accompanies your confession of the gospel of Christ, and for your generosity in sharing with them and with everyone else.

with those money-grubbing "preachers," vaunting themselves as something special (2 Corinthians 11:12, TM).

Paul assured them of his love. He probably did not accept pay from any church while he was there (Acts 20:33-34; 1 Thessalonians 2:6-9) but gratefully accepted help after a church was established and he had left (Philippians 4:10-19). (Paul had thanked the Philippians for the gifts with this assurance: *They are a fragrant offering, an acceptable sacrifice, pleasing to God. And my God will meet all your needs according to his glorious riches in Christ Jesus* (verses 18-19.)

The Corinthian believers were probably relatively well off. The Macedonian churches were extremely poor yet gave *even beyond their ability* (2 Corinthians 8:3) for Jerusalem, and now they were supplying any needs of Paul beyond what he could earn as a tentmaker.

Isn't this true for modern missionaries and new church "planters"? They teach and preach the gospel without charge to those to whom they are taking the message. Prayer and financial support come from established believers "back home" who give to missions and make it possible for those who are called to be able to go and to serve.

4. Do we have a spiritual obligation to prayerfully and financially support those who are establishing a new work for Christ? Record 1 Chronicles 16:23-24.

What was Jesus' instruction to His disciples in Matthew 28:19-20?

What did Jesus promise in Matthew 28:20?

Most of us will not be called by God to *go into all the world and preach the good news* (Mark 16:15), but all of us are called to be a part of taking the gospel *into all the world* with our finances and prayers. And Jesus has told us, *Do not store up for yourselves treasures on earth. . . . But store up for yourselves treasures in heaven. . . . For where your treasure is, there your heart will be also* (Matthew 6:19-21).

5. Write a one-sentence summary of 1 Timothy 6:17-19.

Lord, help me to be among the righteous [who] give without sparing *[Proverbs 21:26] of my finances and my time spent in prayer to spread Your good news to the world. In Jesus' name. Amen.*

The Truth of Christ: Jesus, the Son of God

Reread 2 Corinthians 11:7-12 (concentrating on verse 10) and 1 John 5:5-12.

1. According to verse 10, what did Paul say *is in me*?

This statement by Paul is considered to be an oath affirming his truthfulness; his boasts were not false. Because Paul was finding it necessary to defend himself, in this letter he called on the name of God in this way several times:

1:18—*As surely as God is faithful;*
1:23—*I call God as my witness;*
11:31—*The God and Father of the Lord Jesus . . . knows that I am not lying.*

(Also see Romans 9:1 and Galatians 1:20.)

These oaths were in obedience to the instruction from God to Isaiah: *He who takes an oath in the land will swear by the God of truth* (65:16).

We are still required to give just such an oath if we appear as a witness in a court of law: "I swear to tell the truth, the whole truth, and nothing but the truth, so help me God." If we take on the responsibility of a government position, we swear an oath of honesty in office, most often while placing one hand on the Bible.

God's Word tells us that Jesus Christ was *full of grace and truth* and that *grace and truth came through Jesus Christ* (John 1:14, 17). As followers of Christ, we want the truthfulness of Christ to be reflected in our lives; we want everything we say and the way we live to be totally truthful and honest. But let's look at *The truth of Christ is in me* (2 Corinthians 11:10) in a different sense. We must also know the truth of who Jesus Christ is—the Son of God—and that truth must be "in" us, so deeply embedded that nothing could ever shake our faith. For if we truly know and accept the truth of who Jesus is, place our belief in Him, and accept Him as Savior, we don't just "know about" Jesus—we "know" Jesus. And there is an eternal difference between "knowing about" and "knowing." Are you able to say, *Surely . . . the truth of Christ is in me*?

Many books and articles have been written and countless sermons preached about Jesus. When these are grounded in the Word of God, they are helpful for Christian growth and maturity. But any teaching that contradicts, waters down, or distorts the Word of God is false. For the basic, fundamental source of our beliefs about Jesus Christ, we must read, study, and meditate on God's Word ourselves, *for the foolishness of God is wiser than man's wisdom* (1 Corinthians 1:25).

2. Do you believe the Word of God? If you have Lesson 6, reread your answers to Question 4 on Day 5, describing God's Word. Record a summary of the statements that most accurately reflect your own beliefs (or write your own thoughts) concerning the truthfulness of the Bible.

Who is Jesus Christ? The *wisdom of the world* (1 Corinthians 1:20) often describes Him as a good teacher and moral example. A public figure recently described Jesus in this manner:

> Christ was someone who sought out people who were disenfranchised, people who were left behind. He fought against self-righteousness of people who had everything. He was a person who set an extraordinary example that has lasted 2,000 years, which is pretty inspiring when you think about.

This statement is true as far as it goes—but far from the *whole* truth! This is more a statement of "head knowledge—knowing about Jesus"—than it is of "heart knowledge," or "knowing Jesus."

This is how syndicated columnist Cal Thomas responded to the statement about Jesus:

> If that is all Jesus was (or is), then He is just another entry in *Bartlett's Familiar Quotations*, to be read or not, according to one's inspirational need.
>
> C. S. Lewis brilliantly dealt with this watered-down view of Jesus and what He did in the book *Mere Christianity*. Said Lewis . . . "I'm trying here to prevent anyone from saying the really foolish thing that people often say about Him: 'I'm ready to accept Jesus as a great moral teacher, but I can't accept His claim to be God.' That is the one thing we must not say. A man who was merely a man and said the sort of things Jesus said would not be a great moral teacher. He would either be a lunatic—on a level with a man who says he is a poached egg—or else he would be the Devil of Hell. You must make our choice. Either this man was, and is, the Son of God—or else a madman or something worse."[1]

What is the *wisdom of God* (1 Corinthians 1:21) about Jesus as found in the Word of God? (There is far more scripture about Jesus than space will permit in these lessons.)

3. Is Jesus truly the Son of God? *It is the Spirit who testifies* that Jesus Christ is the Son of God because _____ _____ _____ _____ (1 John 5:6).

4. What did Jesus tell us about the Spirit of truth in the following verses?

John 14:17

John 16:13

Is the Spirit of truth living in you so that He can guide you into all truth?

5. Personalize 1 John 5:11-12.

For the rest of Lesson 8 we will continue this study of *the truth of Christ—the gospel [God] promised beforehand through the prophets in the Holy Scriptures regarding his Son, who as to his human nature was a descendant of David, and who through the Spirit of holiness was declared with power to be the Son of God by his resurrection from the dead: Jesus Christ our Lord* (Romans 1:2-4).

MEMORY CHALLENGE

Read 2 Corinthians 9:13 aloud several times.

DAY THREE

The Truth of Christ: The Word Was God

Read 2 Corinthians 10:12-18 and John 1:1-18.

It is a difficult concept for the finite human mind to fully understand: Jesus—the Word—was not part God and part man but was and is both fully God and fully man. He became fully human but was and is eternal God.

1. Complete these sentences from John 1:

   In the beginning was _____ _____, _____

   _____ _____ _____ _____ _____,

   _____ _____ _____ _____ _____
   (verse 1).

   Through him _____ _____ _____
   _____ (verse 3).

   In him _____ _____, _____ _____

   _____ _____ _____ _____ _____
   _____ (verse 4).

   To all who received him, to those who believed in his
   name, _____ _____ _____ _____

   _____ _____ _____ _____ _____
   (verse 12).

   The Word became _____ _____ _____

   _____ _____ _____ _____ (verse 14).

2. How does John refer to Jesus in verses 14 and 18?

3. He came from the _____ (verse 14) and is at the _____ _____ (verse 18).

As we learn from the first chapter of John, Jesus was truly human and lived on earth as a man, yet He also was always truly God—the eternal Creator. We probably will not be able to fully *understand* this truth about Christ, but unless we can *believe* it, we cannot have sufficient faith to accept Him as Savior and trust *that whoever believes in him shall not perish but have eternal life* (John 3:16).

He is the image of the invisible God, the firstborn over all creation. For by him all things were created . . . all things were created by him and for him. He is before all things, and in him all things hold together. . . . For God was pleased to have all his fullness dwell in him (Colossians 1:15-17, 19).

4. Record Colossians 2:9.

About the Son [God] says, "Your throne, O God, will last forever and ever" (Hebrews 1:8). *He also says, "In the beginning, O Lord, you laid the foundations of the earth, and the heavens are the work of your hands. They will perish, but you remain; they will all wear out like a garment . . . like a garment they will be changed, but you will remain the same, and your years will never end"* (Hebrews 1:10-12).

5. Record Hebrews 13:8.

Jesus is eternal! He was *in the beginning*. He dwells in the hearts of His believing children *in the present*! He will reign as King of Kings and Lord of Lords (Revelation 19:16) in the glorious *future*!

6. What do the following verses say about the eternal nature of Jesus?

   Matthew 28:20

   Hebrews 1:2

   1 Peter 3:22

John 1:14 refers to Christ as *the One and Only, who came from the Father*. Jesus is God's one and only Son, given by God to save a world He loves (John 3:16-17). "Jesus is one of a kind and enjoys a relationship with God unlike all believers who are called 'children' and said to be 'born of God."[1]

7. From the following verses, describe what was occurring when a *voice from heaven [the cloud] said, "This is my Son, whom I love; with him I am well pleased."*

Matthew 3:16-17

Matthew 17:1-5

During Jesus' earthly ministry, most of the religious establishment of the day denied Jesus' claim that He was the Son of God and called Him a blasphemer. Demons, however, *did* recognize that He was the Son of God, including the evil spirit that dwelled in the man who lived in the tombs (Mark 5:1-9) and the demons that *came out of many people shouting, "You are the Son of God!"* . . . *because they knew he was the Christ* (Luke 4:41). Even the Roman centurion and those with him standing guard at the Cross when Jesus was crucified declared, *Surely he was the Son of God!* (Matthew 27:54).

8. Record the words of Jesus in the following verses:

John 12:44-45

John 14:7

We have seen and testify that the Father has sent his Son to be the Savior of the world. If anyone acknowledges that Jesus is the Son of God, God lives in him and he in God (1 John 4:14-16).

Do you believe that Jesus is the Son of God?

Do you *know* Jesus, the Son of God?

MEMORY CHALLENGE

Try to memorize the first phrase: *Because of the service by which you have proved yourself . . .*

DAY FOUR

The Truth of Christ: The Word Became Flesh

Reread 2 Corinthians 11:3-4 and Isaiah 53:1-12.

So the Word became human and lived here on earth among us (John 1:14, NLT).

The Birth of Jesus

1. Record the following verses of prophecy:

Isaiah 7:14

(This prophecy is considered to have a double fulfillment—for the time of Isaiah and for the prophecy of a Messiah. In fact, Matthew [1:23] quotes the verse to indicate fulfillment of this prophecy in the birth of Christ.)

Isaiah 9:6

2. Read Matthew 1:18-27. According to verse 20, why did the angel of the Lord tell Joseph not to be afraid to take Mary as his wife?

What was Joseph told to name the child, and why?

(Jesus means "the Lord saves.")

3. Read Luke 1:26-37. How is Mary described in verse 27?

What did the angel Gabriel say to Mary in verse 31?

What did Mary ask the angel in verse 34?

What was the angel's reply in verse 35?

The Early Years

4. Read Luke 2:21-40. Who were the two people in the Temple who spoke to Joseph and Mary, and what had God revealed to them about the baby Jesus?

Circumcision was required by Jewish law on the eighth day after the birth of a boy (Leviticus 12:3), and he was given his name at that time. A firstborn son was presented to God one month after his birth to be consecrated to the Lord, "redeemed" or "bought back" from God through an offering from his parents (Exodus 13:2, 11-16). Mary and Joseph, Jesus' earthly parents, carried out all the ceremony required after a baby's birth by the law of the Lord (see Luke 2:21-24). "Jesus was not born above the law; instead, he fulfilled it perfectly."[1]

5. Read Luke 2:41-52. How old was Jesus at this time?

What was He doing? Summarize verses 46-47.

The Man Jesus as an Adult

6. Read Luke 4:1-13. Temptation is part of the human experience, and Jesus was tempted—and this was after He had fasted for 40 days and was weak and hungry. What "weapon" (2 Corinthians 10:4) did Jesus use from the "armor of God" (Ephesians 6:11-17) to answer the devil?

Jesus encountered a great deal of accusation, criticism, and unbelief. *Even his own brothers did not believe in him* (John 7:5). He experienced grief (Matthew 14:1-13; John 11:32-35) and betrayal (Mark 14:41-46). *The Son of Man has no place to lay his head* (Matthew 8:20).

To some of the Pharisees and teachers who had asked for a miraculous sign to prove He was the Son of God, Jesus said, *The Son of Man will be three days and three nights in the heart of the earth* (Matthew 12:40). Jesus knew that He was to be put to death, explaining that to His disciples at least three times during His ministry (Matthew 16:21; 17:22-23; 20:17-19) and again just before His arrest (Matthew 26:36-45).

Having become human, he stayed human. It was an incredibly humbling process. He didn't claim special privileges. Instead, he lived a selfless, obedient life and then died a selfless, obedient death—and the worst kind of death at that—a crucifixion (Philippians 2:8, TM).

7. Summarize Luke 23:44-46.

Jesus was put to death, but as one preacher told his congregation in a Good Friday sermon: "Today may be Friday—but Sunday's a'comin'!"

We have a great High Priest who has gone to heaven, Jesus the Son of God. Let us cling to him and never stop trusting him. This High Priest of ours understands our weaknesses, for he faced all of the same temptations we do, yet he did not sin. So let us come boldly to the throne of our gracious God. There we will receive his mercy, and we will find grace to help us when we need it (Hebrews 4:14-16, NLT).

MEMORY CHALLENGE

Work today on memorizing the second phrase: *men will praise God for the obedience that accompanies your confession of the gospel of Christ.*

The Truth of Christ: The Risen Lord!

Read Mark 16:1-17.

(For more in-depth accounts of these events, read John 20:1-20 and Luke 24:13-40.)

HIS RESURRECTION—*He was crucified in weakness, yet he lives by God's power* (2 Corinthians 13:4).

1. According to Mark 16:4-5, what did the women find when they went to the tomb on the first day of the week?

What did the man tell the women?

According to verse 9, to whom did Jesus first appear?

According to verses 12 and 14, to whom did Jesus appear next?

Why did Jesus rebuke the Eleven?

2. Read John 20:24-29, and record the words of Jesus in verse 29.

3. Jesus appeared a third time to some of the disciples while they were fishing (John 21:1-14). To whom did Jesus appear according to 1 Corinthians 15:6-7?

He showed himself to [the apostles] and gave many convincing proofs that he was alive. He appeared to them over a period of forty days (Acts 1:3).

HIS ASCENSION—*After the Lord Jesus had spoken to them, he was taken up into heaven and he sat at the right hand of God* (Mark 16:19).

4. Paul said, *and last of all he appeared to me also* (1 Corinthians 15:8). Read Acts 9:1-7. Explain (briefly) what happened to Saul (Paul) as he was on his journey to Damascus (verses 3-5).

About 60 years later, when John was in the Spirit, Jesus appeared and told him, *Do not be afraid. I am the First and the Last. I am the Living One; I was dead, and behold I am alive for ever and ever!* (Revelation 1:9, 17-18).

HIS RETURN—After Jesus was taken up, *Two men dressed in white told the disciples, "This same Jesus, who has been taken from you into heaven, will come back in the same way you have seen him go into heaven"* (Acts 1:10-11). *Look, he is coming with the clouds, and every eye will see him* (Revelation 1:7).

5. Summarize the following verses:

Mark 13:26-27

1 Thessalonians 4:16-17

The grace of God that brings salvation has appeared to all men. It teaches us to say "No" to ungodliness and worldly passions, and to live self-controlled, upright and godly lives in this present age, while we wait for the blessed hope—the glorious returning of our great God and Savior, Jesus Christ (Titus 2:11-13).

Memorize the last phrase today: *and for your generosity in sharing with them and with everyone else.*

DAY SIX

The Truth of Christ: Our Lord and Savior

Read 1 John 2:1-6, 21-25.

1. According to verses 1-2, who is the atoning sacrifice for our sins?

2. According to verse 22, who is the liar?

How can we know the way? Jesus answered, "I am the way and the truth and the life. No one comes to the Father except through me" (John 14:5-6).

We have all read and heard them—the denials that Jesus is the only way to God. A professor from a university religious studies department made this statement recently: "Many evangelical Christians . . . may have been taught that Christianity is the best religion—and are now being told that other faiths are equally valid. . . . My job is to make each of the religions come alive."[1] You have heard comments such as these on television talk shows: "There are many paths to God. The important thing is that you believe something"; "It is narrow-minded bigotry to tell others that they must believe in Jesus to be acceptable to God"; "A loving God would not condemn anyone to eternal punishment."

3. Jesus said, *No one comes to the Father except through me.* Record the following verses:

John 3:36

1 John 2:23

From the earliest Old Testament times, the blood sacrifice of innocent unblemished animals had been required for forgiveness of sins. "The offering of blood had a twofold significance also—it was a representation of the pure life which the sinner should have; and that atonement could be [provided] through death only. Furthermore, the animal sacrifices pointed to Christ as the . . . Lamb of God whose blood alone could take away the sin of the world."[2] *For God made Christ, who never sinned, to be the offering for our sin, so that we could be made right with God through Christ* (2 Corinthians 5:21, NLT).

"The conception of Christ's atoning sacrifice as found in the New Testament is simply the completion of that which was foreshadowed in the Old Testament. . . . He laid His life down voluntarily, for no one had the power to take it from Him. Hence, we must regard the crucifixion as not merely an event brought about by circumstances, but as the great end for which He came into the world."[3]

4. Are you able to say, *Surely the truth of Christ is in me?* (2 Corinthians 11:10). Personalize 1 John 1:9.

Would you like to accept Jesus Christ as your Savior? Ask your small group to pray with you.

From the beginning God chose you to be saved through the sanctifying work of the Spirit and through belief in the truth (2 Thessalonians 2:13). *God . . . loved us and sent his Son as an atoning sacrifice for our sins. . . . And we have seen and testify that the Father has sent his Son to be the Savior of the world* (1 John 4:10, 14). *If we walk in the light, as he is in the light . . . the blood of Jesus, his Son, purifies us from all sin* (1 John 1:7).

MEMORY CHALLENGE

Try to put the phrases together and be able to quote 2 Corinthians 9:13 with your small group.

2 Corinthians

■ A Study of 2 Corinthians 11—12

Masquerade

Read 2 Corinthians 11, concentrating on verses 13-15.

1. How did Paul refer to the *super-apostles* (verse 5) in verse 13?

2. Satan masquerades (disguises himself) as an _____

   _____ _____ (verse 14).
   Satan's servants, the false prophets, masquerade as

   _____ _____ _____ (verse 15).

3. What will their end be?

4. How are false prophets described in 2 Peter 2:17, and what will be their fate?

5. What will the false prophets do, and what will be their end according to 2 Peter 2:1?

6. Satan doesn't present himself to us as himself, the *prince of the dominion of darkness* (Colossians 1:13) and the power *of this dark world* (Ephesians 6:12), but disguises himself as *an angel of light*. How did Jesus describe the devil, Satan, in John 8:44?

In the same way, Satan's *servants masquerade as servants of righteousness*. We can be deceived by Satan and his servants, who may appear attractive, good, and moral. They may even quote carefully selected verses from Scripture—usually out of context. Be careful that you do not allow an impressive appearance or smooth talk fool you into believing that a fake teacher is a true follower of Christ.

Is it possible for Christians to be led stray by false teachings? Yes! False teachers offer "proofs" and arguments that sound convincing if you are not armed with knowledge and understanding of scriptural truth.

7. Summarize the warnings found in the following verses:

   Matthew 7:15-16

   Mark 13:22-23

   Acts 20:30-31

2 Corinthians 9:14

In their prayers for you their hearts will go out to you, because of the surpassing grace God has given you.

1 Timothy 4:1-2

How can we identify those who *masquerade as servants of righteousness*? Jesus said, *By their fruit you will recognize them* (Matthew 7:16, 20).

- They try to discredit true Christian preachers and teachers. The false teachers in Corinth had tried to discredit Paul, his ministry, and his authority.
- They are self-serving and often power-hungry and overbearing (2 Corinthians 11:20), boastful (verse 18), and/or greedy (2:17). They focus more attention on themselves than on Christ.
- They cause divisions and conflicts in the church. Paul said, *Keep away from them* (Romans 16:17).
- They preach or teach a message that is not the true gospel of the Bible (2 Corinthians 11:4). They de-emphasize the divine nature of Christ or the inspiration of the Bible.
- Their lifestyle is not consistent with biblical morality (Matthew 12:33-35).
- They urge believers to make decisions based more on human judgment than on prayer and biblical guidelines.[1]

One final word of counsel, friends. Keep a sharp eye out for those who take bits and pieces of the teaching that you learned and then use them to make trouble. Give these people a wide berth. They have no intention of living for our Master Christ. They're only in this for what they can get out of it, and aren't above using pious sweet-talk to dupe unsuspecting innocents (Romans 16:17-18, TM).

Unscrupulous con men will continue to exploit the faith. They're as deceived as the people they lead astray. As long as they are out there, things can only get worse. But don't let it faze you. . . . There's nothing like the written Word of God for showing you the way to salvation through faith in Christ Jesus. Every part of Scripture is God-breathed and useful one way or another—showing us truth, exposing our rebellion, correcting our mistakes, training us to live God's way. Through the Word we are put together and shaped up for the tasks God has for us (2 Timothy 3:13-17, TM).

DAY TWO

Foolish Boasting

Read 2 Corinthians 11:16-23.

Paul begins his "fool's speech" (11:16—12:13), where he boasts of his credentials (11:22-23), his sufferings as an apostle (11:23-29), his "visions and revelations" (12:1-6), and his mighty works (12:12). He was speaking ironically because he was reluctant and embarrassed to be boasting in this way.* "He does not let us forget that he is effecting the role of a fool in order to make a rhetorical point about his opponents."[1]

1. Paul said that he was talking *as a fool*, not as _____
_____ _____.

2. Why would Paul be talking *as a fool* by boasting? Refer to 2 Corinthians 10:17-18.

3. According to 11:12, 18, why, then, did Paul say that he would boast?

Paul had introduced the gospel of Jesus Christ to these Corinthians, and they had accepted Christ through his ministry. Because his authority as an apostle had been challenged by the false teachers, the faith of the Corinthian believers was in danger of being compromised or destroyed.

4. Read 2 Corinthians 11:1-4. According to verses 3-4, why did Paul hope the Corinthians would *put up with a little of [his] foolishness*?

5. Paul accused the Corinthians of being willing to *put up with fools since you are so wise* (11:19). What else were the Christians in Corinth willing to *put up with* from the false teachers?

The false teachers had tried to enslave the Corinthians to their will by forcing them to submit to circumcision and to obey the Jewish laws, thereby abandoning the glorious freedom of the gospel of grace. And they *exploited* the Corinthians. The Greek word translated "exploit" was commonly used to describe how animals devour their prey. They allowed the false teachers to devour their resources "like parasites."[2]

The Greek word translated "takes advantage" was a word used to describe how a hunter traps an animal or bird. The false teachers had taken them in, ensnared them, as a hunter captures his or her prey.

Anyone who pushes himself or herself forward exalts himself or herself. The Greek word literally means "to lift on high." Paul's opponents were arrogant, exalting themselves not only over Paul but against God himself.

6. What did Jesus say in Matthew 23:12 about the one who exalts himself or herself?

The phrase *slaps you in the face* (verse 20) may be figurative, referring to insulting speech or behavior, or it might have been actual slaps in the face. In the first century it was not uncommon for religious authorities to slap the face of a blasphemer. Paul was struck on the mouth when he was brought before the chief priests and the Sanhedrin (Acts 23:2). "Apparently these false teachers had concentrated their power in Corinth, so much so that they had the audacity to slap those who opposed them."[3] Paul told the Corinthians that he was "too weak" to use such un-Christlike behavior against them.

7. False teachers and preachers with charisma continue to ensnare, exploit, and enslave their followers today. Jesus warned us, *Watch out that no one deceives you* (Matthew 24:4). What did he tell us about the end of this age in Matthew 24:10-13?

According to verse 13, who will be saved?

Record Hebrews 13:9.

Dear friends, do not believe everyone who claims to speak by the Spirit. You must test them to see if the spirit they have comes from God. For there are many false prophets in the world. . . .

But you belong to God, my dear children. You have already won your fight with these false prophets, because the Spirit who lives in you is greater than the spirit who lives in the world. These people belong to this world, so they speak from the world's viewpoint, and the world listens to them. But we belong to God (1 John 4:1, 4-6, NLT).

And that about wraps it up. God is strong, and he wants you strong. So take everything the Master has set out for you, well-made weapons of the best materials. And put them to use so you will be able to stand up to everything the Devil throws your way. This is no afternoon athletic contest that we'll walk away from and forget about in a couple of hours. This is for keeps, a life or death fight to the finish against the Devil and all his angels.

Be prepared. You're up against more than you can handle on your own. Take all the help you can get, every weapon God has issued, so that when it's all over but the shouting you'll still be on your feet. Truth, righteousness, peace, faith, and salvation are more than words. Learn to apply them. You'll need them throughout your life. God's Word is an indispensable weapon. Pray hard and long (Ephesians 6:10-18, TM).

Share with your family your love for and belief in the Word of God. Teach your children to put their trust in God and to obey Him. And pray for their protection!

*"'Ironic' applies to a humorous or sarcastic form of expression in which the intended meaning of what is said is directly opposite to the usual sense" (Webster's New World College Dictionary, Fourth Edition, 1272).

MEMORY CHALLENGE

Why will their (the believers in Judea) hearts go out to you (the Corinthians)?

Trials

Read 2 Corinthians 11:21-30.

1. The false teachers had boasted of their superior credentials. Paul told the Corinthians that he was not *in the least inferior to those "super-apostles"* (11:5), and he, too, could boast. Of what did Paul boast in verses 22-23?

Even though Paul felt foolish in doing so, in order to refute the charges made against him by the false teachers, he presented his credentials. Apparently, because he had been born a Roman citizen in Tarsus rather than Palestine, he had been accused of not being a real Jew.

Hebrews were considered to be Jews who were able to speak and read Hebrew and/or Aramaic, the language of Palestine. Many of the Jews in Greece were able to speak only Greek, but Paul was educated in Jerusalem, and as a former Pharisee, he had been a Hebrew scholar.

Israelites described God's chosen people, probably those who observed all religious and social aspects of being Jews, certainly true of any Pharisee.

Abraham's descendants (which Paul was) were heirs of the promise (see Genesis 12:1-3). Paul may have been born a Roman citizen, but he was a pure Jew.

2. Read Galatians 3:26-29. What is now the only requirement to be Abraham's seed and heir to the promise?

After establishing his religious and racial pedigree, Paul listed the suffering, trials, and humiliations he had endured and the constant dangers he had faced as a *servant of Christ.* "The persecutions, the poverty, the scourgings, the hunger, and the nakedness of which Paul had boasted were not the things in which men of the world pride themselves or that commonly attract human applause."[1] Instead of boasting about his abilities and accomplishments, Paul pointed out how God had worked through his suffering and weakness.

3. Read 2 Corinthians 1:8-10. In verse 9, what reason did Paul give for the hardships he had suffered?

What had God done for Paul, and what was Paul's hope that He would continue to do?

4. *Besides everything else* (2 Corinthians 11:28), what pressure had Paul faced daily?

Paul's "greatest burden was not *around* him but *within* him: the care of the churches . . . because he identified with the believers (verse 29). Whatever happened to 'his children' touched his own heart and he could not abandon them."[2]

Paul prayed for the churches and asked them to pray for him. Pray daily for your pastor. He or she faces *daily the pressure of [his or her] concern for* your church—administrative, financial, emotional, and spiritual concerns.

5. In many areas of the world today Christians still suffer intense persecution of all kinds as servants of Christ, while most of us are far more apt to suffer ridicule, discrimination, or perhaps some hostility, in Christ's name. Peter said not to be *surprised at the painful trial you are suffering.* Read 1 Peter 4:12-19, and summarize verse 13.

If you are insulted because of the name of Christ, you are blessed (verse 14). *If you suffer as a Christian, do not be ashamed*, but do what? (See verse 16.)

According to verse 19, what else should *those who suffer according to God's will* do?

6. What are our momentary trials achieving for us, according to 2 Corinthians 4:17?

7. Are you going through a time of trial? King David experienced God's sustaining grace and deliverance in the midst of his troubles. Personalize the following verses:

Psalm 9:9

Psalm 34:17

Psalm 145:14

8. Read and meditate on Psalm 91. Personalize a verse that is especially meaningful to you.

"Because I love Him, the Lord will rescue me. He will protect me, for I acknowledge His name. I will call upon Him, and He will answer me; He will be with me in trouble, He will deliver me and honor me" (Psalm 91:14-15, NIV, personalized).

But now, God's Message . . .
Don't be afraid, I've redeemed you.
    I've called your name. You're mine.
When you're in over your head, I'll be there with you.
    When you're in rough waters, you will not go down.
When you're in between a rock and a hard place,
    it won't be a dead end—
Because I am God, your personal God,
    The Holy of Israel, your Savior.
I have paid a huge price for you: . . .
    That's how much you mean to me!
That's how much I love you!

(Isaiah 43:1-4, TM)

MEMORY CHALLENGE

When will their hearts *go out to you?*

DAY FOUR

My Grace Is Sufficient

Read 2 Corinthians 12:1-10.

Paul was speaking of himself when he wrote that he knew *a man in Christ who . . . was caught up to the third heaven. Whether it was in the body or out of the body* [in his spirit] *I do not know—God knows.* Perhaps it was when he was stoned and left for dead (see Acts 14:19-20). What Paul was certain of was that he had *heard inexpressible things* and had been touched by God.

1. According to verse 7, what was given Paul to keep him *from becoming conceited*?

2. What did Paul say that he did three times?

3. What was the Lord's answer to Paul?

Paul believed that God had allowed a *messenger of Satan* to afflict him with *a thorn in my flesh* to keep him from *becoming conceited* as a result of the visions and revelations from the Lord that he had experienced. Most modern Bible interpreters believe that Paul's "thorn" was probably a chronic and debilitating, or recurring, physical ailment, but no one really knows what it was. And that allows each of us to be able to apply God's promise to Paul—*My grace is sufficient*—to our own "thorn," whatever it may be.

When God permits suffering to come into your life, how do you deal with it? Do you become bitter and blame God? Do you just give up and become resigned to it without allowing God's blessings into your life? Or do you put on a brave front, determined to endure it in your own strength? This is what Paul did: He prayed for healing "three times," but when the Lord said "no," Paul accepted His will and allowed the strength of the risen Christ to be revealed through his life and ministry.

4. *The Lord* with whom Paul pleaded was Christ Jesus. Why did Paul plead *three times*? He didn't say. Perhaps he was thinking of Jesus, who asked God three times, *If it is possible, may this cup be taken from me* (Matthew 26:36-44). Record the words of Jesus that followed that plea (verses 39, 42).

The most effective argument that Paul's opponents had used against him probably was his weakness, but Paul saw it as a gift from God. "The Lord knows how to balance our lives. If we have only blessings, we may become proud; so he permits us to have burdens as well."[1]

When you are in the midst of a trial, it may seem difficult to look at it as a gift, but a trial can be an instrument that God can use to build godly character. "When you walk along the shore of an ocean, you notice that the rocks are sharp in the quiet coves, but polished in those places where the waves beat against them. God can use the 'waves and billows' of life to polish us if we will let Him."[2]

A family member of mine currently suffers from a chronic, debilitating, and progressive disease. He has been anointed, and family and friends have prayed with him for his healing (see James 5:14-15), but the *prayer offered in faith* has not made his body whole. He told me recently that God has not given him a promise of healing, but He has promised that His grace would be sufficient. I frequently see the marks of pain in his face and always the increasing weakness of his body, but his smile and testimony witness to the "sufficient grace" of God at work in his life.

No, we don't always receive instant healing or respite from trouble in answer to our prayers. But if we accept God's will and open our lives to His grace, His strength, and His power in the midst of our weakness, His grace will be sufficient—sufficient for every need, every trial, every temptation—for anything we might face in this life. His grace is sufficient for you!

So let us come boldly to the throne of our gracious God. There we will receive his mercy, and we will find grace to help us when we need it (Hebrews 4:16, NLT).

MEMORY CHALLENGE

What did Paul mean by *the surpassing grace God has given you*? Refer to 2 Corinthians 8:7; 9:8.

DAY FIVE

Power in Weakness

Read 2 Corinthians 12:7-10.

1. Paul said, *I will boast all the more gladly about my weaknesses* (verse 9). Why?

For when I am _____, then I am _____ (verse 10).

Paul's opponents in Corinth boasted about what they considered to be their superior strengths—their recommendations, their Jewish heritage, their speaking ability, and their wisdom; but Paul "boasted" about his weaknesses. It was through Paul's weakness that God was able to fill him with His power and make him strong. We also must not rely on our own strengths, talents, energy, or efforts. We must instead rely on God and His power to make us "effective for Him . . . and help us do work that has lasting value."[1]

God permits us to become weak so that we might receive His power and strength. It is only when we are weak and emptied of self that we can then be filled with God so that His power can be revealed most fully in us.

2. How may we achieve peace in the midst of trial, according to Isaiah 26:3-4?

3. What assurance did Jesus give us in John 16:33?

4. Psalm 68:35 tells us that God *gives power and strength to his people*. Record Philippians 4:13.

5. Personalize the following promises:

Deuteronomy 31:8

Isaiah 41:13

Romans 8:28

We pray that you'll have the strength to stick it out over the long haul—not the grim strength of gritting your teeth but the glory-strength God gives. It is strength that endures the unendurable and spills over into joy, thanking the Father who makes us strong enough to take part in everything bright and beautiful that he has for us (Colossians 1:11-12, TM).

MEMORY CHALLENGE

Fill in the blanks:

In their _____ for you their _____ will go out to you, because of the _____ _____ God has given you.

2 Corinthians 9:14

DAY SIX

For Your Strengthening

Read 2 Corinthians 12:11-21.

Paul is preparing to make his third visit to Corinth. On his first visit he introduced them to the gospel (Acts 18:1-18). The second time was the *painful visit* (2 Corinthians 2:1). Paul does not want the third visit to be another painful experience for them and for him; so once again he addresses the problems in the church.

1. In verse 11, what did Paul say the Corinthians *ought to have done*?

Paul scolded them for their lack of appreciation. They *ought to have* been boasting about him (instead of compelling him to boast) and defending him from the malicious rumors about him that were circulating in the church.

Paul had been an instrument through whom God had demonstrated His powers.* Signs and wonders are qualities of the miracles of God. "Signs" are not for empty show but for our instruction. "Wonders" arouse us to great astonishment. "Miracles" are evidences of God's divine power, something not seen in the ordinary course of our lives.[1]

2. Paul had not been a burden to the Corinthians. In verse 14, why did he say he would not be a burden to them on the third trip?

Paul compared himself to a parent caring for his or her children. (He is referring here to very young children—as the Corinthians were spiritually—not grown children with elderly parents needing assistance.)

3. According to verse 15, instead of being a burden, what will Paul do?

How could you show your appreciation to your pastor and Sunday School teacher for their spiritual commitment of time and resources?

Apparently some of the Corinthians were really bothered by the fact that Paul refused payment for his ministry. This unrest was probably stirred up by the false teachers, who were on the defensive because they were exploiting the church financially. But Paul did not want their money—he wanted *them*. He wanted to present the church *as a pure virgin* to Christ (11:2).

4. Now we come to the real reason for Paul's defense of himself and his ministry. Was Paul's defense for himself? Summarize 1 Corinthians 4:3-4.

In 2 Corinthians 12:19, what reason did Paul give for speaking to them in this way?

Paul feared that he would not find the church to be in the right condition spiritually and would be forced to be very stern with them (verse 20). He listed sins of behavior that had weakened the church by disrupting worship or contributing to disunity (verse 20). These sins of pride cause disunity in our churches today, and too often they are not properly condemned and disciplined.

5. After repentance for these sins, in one word (according to 1 Corinthians 13) what is *the most excellent way* (1 Corinthians 12:31) of removing discord from the church?

The sins listed in 2 Corinthians 12:21 are sexual sins. The immoral culture of Corinth had been allowed to infiltrate the church. We, too, must guard vigilantly to keep the immorality of our culture from infiltrating our churches. "Sin in the church is like cancer in the human body; it must be cut out."[2]

*Some of the miracles of Paul are mentioned or recorded in the Book of Acts: 13:6-12; 14:1-3; 14:8-10; 15:12; 16:16-18; 19:11-12; 20:9-12. Paul himself was miraculously delivered as well: 14:19-20; 16:25-28; 28:1-10.

MEMORY CHALLENGE

Be prepared to say 2 Corinthians 9:14 from memory with your group.

2 Corinthians LESSON 10

■ A Study of 2 Corinthians 13

DAY ONE

Warning!

Read 2 Corinthians 13, concentrating on verses 1-4.

1. Paul was writing to the Corinthians in preparation for his _____ visit.

2. What warning had Paul given the Corinthians on his second visit that he repeats in this letter (verse 2)?

This was not a personal power struggle; the very salvation of these Corinthian believers was at stake. So Paul warned the Corinthians that they would face strong disciplinary action from him on this next visit if they remained unrepentant. He had expressed his love for them, he had addressed their accusations against him, and he had given them time to repent. Now he warns them sternly that the time has come to use his authority as an apostle to administer the necessary discipline on this visit. But Paul is still hopeful that they will correct the situation before his next visit.

3. According to verse 1, by what means must every matter be established?

Paul quoted this instruction from Deuteronomy 19:15. Record verse 15.

This principle regarding judgment had been followed throughout Old Testament history and had been approved by Jesus (John 8:17); Paul applied it here to the New Testament Church. He instructed Timothy not to *entertain an*

accusation against an elder unless it is brought by two or three witnesses (1 Timothy 5:19). In 1 John 5:7-8 we learn that there are three witnesses who testify that Jesus is the Son of God: *the Spirit, the water and the blood; and the three are in agreement.*

What is the *matter* that *must be established*? There are two possibilities, and perhaps Paul was referring to both of them:

- Paul's apostleship had been challenged by his opponents on his second visit to Corinth. He had been seriously offended, and the rest of the congregation had apparently done nothing in response. He was sending Titus and another brother ahead to collect the offering (8:17-18); they would be able to witness to the authenticity of Paul's apostleship, as would any of the Macedonian believers who might be with Paul when he visited Corinth this next time (9:4).
- Paul was afraid that when he arrived again in Corinth he would find that they were still tolerating sin in the church (12:20-21), and he wanted *every matter* concerning the sinners to *be established* according to biblical principles.

4. Christ *was crucified in* _____, *yet he lives by* _____ _____ (2 Corinthians 13:4).

What was the Lord's assurance to Paul concerning his weakness (12:9)?

MEMORY CHALLENGE

2 Corinthians 9:15

Thanks be to God for his indescribable gift!

Paul explained once again that his *weakness* in the eyes of his opponents was not a legitimate argument against his authority and apostleship. He had been invested with the power of the resurrected Lord to serve Him as His apostle.

Paul's opponents were *demanding proof that Christ [was] speaking through* Paul, and since they had rejected the evidence that he had given them through his words and his life, he would bring them "proof." And they probably wouldn't like it! Now they would get the decisiveness and authoritarianism they were seeking; Paul would *not spare those who sinned earlier or any of the others* (2 Corinthians 13:2). "Stern discipline will be a sure sign that through Paul's ministry Christ is *not weak* toward them but is *mighty* in them (cf. Rom. 15:18)."[1]

5. How should we treat rebellious false teachers and their followers, and why should we treat them this way, according to the following verses?

Titus 1:13 (Read verses 10-14.)

2 John 10-11 (Read verses 9-11.)

6. Paul had the authority to put an unrepentant sinner out of the church for the sake of maintaining the purity of the church. Jesus gave His followers guidelines to follow when a fellow Christian *sins against you*. It would also be appropriate to follow these guidelines in the church before taking such drastic action as putting out a member. What are the three steps He told us to follow first? (See Matthew 18:15-18.)

7. *Christ loved the church and gave himself up for her* (Ephesians 5:25). Record Revelation 3:19 (the words of the risen Christ).

8. Summarize 1 Corinthians 5:6-7.

("Yeast" represents sin in the church.)

These are the words of the risen Christ to the church at Sardis: *I know all the things you do, and that you have a reputation for being alive—but you are dead. . . . Your deeds are far from right in the sight of God. Go back to what you heard and believed at first; hold to it firmly and turn to me again. Unless you do, I will come upon you suddenly, as unexpected as a thief* (Revelation 3:2-3, NLT).

Is there sin in your life? *How can you say to your brother, "Let me take the speck out of your eye," when all the time there is a plank in your own eye? You hypocrite, first take the plank out of your own eye, and then you will see clearly to remove the speck from your brother's eye* (Matthew 7:4-5). If there is sin in your life, confess it to Christ; He will forgive your sins and purify you from all unrighteousness (1 John 1:9). And follow the command of Jesus *to leave your life of sin* (John 8:11).

If there is sin in your church, you have several choices. You can ignore it or you can gossip about it; either could damage or even destroy the church. Or you could do what Scripture commands and thereby allow the Spirit of Christ to heal the church and hopefully to restore the sinner. To discipline a church or an individual member is a difficult and painful task for those who are forced to use their authority to take this action because of unrepentant sin. But "true Christian love sometimes demands confrontation."[2]

You shouldn't act as if everything is just fine when one of your Christian companions is promiscuous or crooked, is flip with God or rude to friends, gets drunk or becomes greedy and predatory. You can't just go along with this, treating it as acceptable behavior. I'm not responsible for what the outsiders do, but don't we have some responsibility for those within our community of believers? God decides on the outsiders, but we need to decide when our brothers and sisters are out of line and, if necessary, clean house (1 Corinthians 5:11-13, TM).

Pray for your church and its leaders!

Examine Yourselves

Read 2 Corinthians 13:5-10.

1. Why did Paul tell the Corinthians to *examine yourselves*?

   Paul told them: *Do you not realize that Christ Jesus is in you—unless* what?

2. According to verses 7 and 9, what was Paul's prayer for the Corinthian believers?

3. What did Paul say he could not *do anything against*?

4. Why did Paul write these warnings in this letter?

5. What authority had the Lord given Paul? (You will also find this in 10:8.)

One method people use to make themselves seem better than they really are is to condemn someone else. Paul's opponents in Corinth had been finding fault with Paul while ignoring their own sin. "You've been examining me," Paul told them. "Now you need to *examine yourselves*." He reminded them that *Christ Jesus is in you—unless, of course, you fail the test.* If the Corinthians' relationship with Christ was right and was firmly established, they would not resent, but would instead welcome, an honest self-examination.

Paul hoped that if the Corinthians passed the test, they would realize that the *proof that Christ [was] speaking through* Paul (verse 3) was in their own acceptance of Christ and their relationship with Him, which were results of Paul's ministry. Paul's desire for them to pass the test was not so that he might be seen to have *stood the test* but that they might do *what is right*. In fact, if they did the right thing, Paul would not have the need or the opportunity to present the

evidence of the authority of Christ in him that he had threatened to give them (verses 2-3).

Paul preferred that his opponents view him as "weak" and as having failed the test if it meant that the Corinthians passed the test and were strong in their faith. "He is *glad* to lose the opportunity for the legitimate use of his power to punish and thus to prove his strength if it can be due to their moral and spiritual strength."[1] Paul was praying for the perfection of the Corinthian believers—that they might grow in Christ and become more and more spiritually mature.

6. *Christ Jesus is in you* refers to the indwelling presence of Christ in the individual believer as well as in the Church. Personalize the following verses:

   Galatians 2:20

   Ephesians 3:16-17

7. As Christians we need to examine ourselves regularly— have a spiritual checkup. Do you have the witness of the Holy Spirit? Personalize the following verses:

   Romans 8:9

   Romans 8:16

   Do you love your brothers and sisters? What does 1 John 3:10 say about *anyone who does not love his brother*?

   Do you practice righteousness? Record the following verses:

   1 John 2:6

   1 John 3:6

1 John 3:9

(The questions in No. 7 were based on *Be Encouraged*, by Warren W. Wiersbe, 148.)

8. Personalize or summarize the following verses:

1 John 2:3

1 John 2:15

The evidence of Christ in us will also be revealed in our positive actions. What do the following verses teach us to do?

John 15:4

John 15:8

James 2:14-17 (Give a brief summary.)

You may need to ask and answer other questions as you examine yourself. You will need to do thought checks and attitude adjustment checks regularly. If you have any thought, attitude, or action that is displeasing to God, ask Him to forgive you. Ask God, as King David did, to forgive your hidden faults, keep you from willful sin, and make the words of your mouth and the meditation of your heart pleasing in His sight (Psalm 19:12-14).

From your heart, pray these verses daily:
Search me, O God, and know my heart;
test me and know my thoughts.
Point out anything in me that offends you,
and lead me along the path of everlasting life.
                                        (Psalm 139:23-24, NLT)

MEMORY CHALLENGE

What did Paul mean by God's *indescribable gift*?

DAY THREE

Rejoice!

Read 2 Corinthians 13:11-14, concentrating on verse 11.

1. Paul began the closing of this letter to the Corinthians with some admonitions for the church (verse 11). What were they?

These admonitions from Paul to the church at Corinth are still vitally important to the Church today. "These traits do not come to a church by glossing over problems, conflicts, and difficulties. They are not produced by neglect, denial, withdrawal, or bitterness. They are the by-products of the extremely hard work of solving problems."[1] The result of working out our problems in obedience to these admonitions is more than worth the effort: *the God of peace and love will be with you.*

The word that the *New International Version* translates as "good-by" is translated "rejoice" in the *New American Standard Bible* and the *New Living Translation*. It is a Greek word that was used for greetings and farewells, so "good-by" may be correct, but the word literally means and is translated "rejoice," (or "happy" or "glad") throughout this letter (2:3; 6:10; 7:7, 9, 13, 16; 13:9). In Philippians 3:1 a very similar Greek phrase is translated *Finally, my brothers, rejoice in the Lord!*

A church divided into factions, exhibiting quarreling, jealousy, anger, slander, gossip, arrogance, and disorder; and tolerating sexual immorality (12:20-21) has little reason to "rejoice." And "Paul desperately wants the Corinthians to be a cause of his own rejoicing (cf. 2:3; 7:9, 16; 13:9). If the Corinthians repent of their attitude toward the apostle before he arrives, then they have reason for rejoicing—in the Lord, with each other, and with Paul. Rejoicing thus becomes an expression of unity in the congregation."[2]

2. Personalize the reasons for rejoicing according to the following verses:

Nehemiah 8:10 (last phrase)

Psalm 13:5

Psalm 33:21

Luke 10:20

Acts 2:28

Romans 5:11

3. Record Psalm 9:2.

Rejoice, the Lord is King;
 Your Lord and King adore!
Rejoice, give thanks, and sing,
 And triumph evermore.
Lift up your heart; Lift up your voice!
 Rejoice; again I say: rejoice!

Jesus, the Savior, reigns,
 The God of truth and love.
When He had purged our stains,
 He took His seat above.
Lift up your heart; Lift up your voice!
 Rejoice; again I say: rejoice!

His kingdom cannot fail:
 He rules o'er earth and heav'n.
The keys of death and hell
 Are to our Jesus giv'n.
Lift up your heart; Lift up your voice!
 Rejoice; again I say: rejoice!

Rejoice in glorious hope!
 Our Lord, the Judge, shall come
And take His servants up
 To their eternal home.
Lift up your heart; Lift up your voice!
 Rejoice; again I say: rejoice!
    —Charles Wesley

Though you have not seen him, you love him; and even though you do not see him now, you believe in him and are filled with an inexpressible and glorious joy, for you are receiving the goal of your faith, the salvation of your souls (1 Peter 1:8-9).

Rejoice in the Lord always. I will say it again: Rejoice! (Philippians 4:4).

MEMORY CHALLENGE

Today (and every day), thank God often for the *indescribable gift* of His Son, Jesus Christ.

DAY FOUR

Aim for Perfection

Read 2 Corinthians 13:11.

1. What was Paul's instruction after *good-by* ("rejoice")?

Aim for perfection means "Let yourselves be steadily perfect."[1] Paul was urging the Corinthians to grow up into spiritual maturity and to take care of the problems in the church. If a church, or an individual believer, is not growing spiritually, it is disobedience to God's Word and to His will.

Spiritual maturity is a process involving time and growth, trial and development. It continues throughout the life of the believer—growth that results in more faith, more love, more hope, and more patience. "We can encourage this growth process by deliberately applying Scripture to all areas of our lives, by accepting the discipline and guidance Christ provides, and by giving him control of our desires and goals."[2] *If anyone obeys his Word, God's love is truly made complete in him* (1 John 2:5).

2. Personalize the following verses:

   1 Kings 8:61

   2 Peter 3:14 (Read verses 11-14.)

3. Read Colossians 1:21-23. Personalize verses 22-23.

4. Personalize what Paul urges us to do *in view of God's mercy* (Romans 12:1-2).

5. Read 2 Peter 1:5-9. What qualities are we to add to our faith (verses 5-7)?

According to verse 8, why is it important to possess these qualities in our lives as Christians?

The term "Christian perfection" is often misunderstood. Let's take a look at what it does *not* mean:
"1. Christian perfection is not *absolute* perfection. This belongs to God only. . . .
2. It is not *angelic* perfection. The holy angels are unfallen beings [and] . . . are not liable to mistake as is man in his present state of weakness and infirmity. . . .
3. It is not *Adamic* perfection . . . man in his original state [before the fall].
4. It is not perfection in *knowledge*. Not only was man's will perverted, and his affections alienated by the fall, but his intellect was darkened. . . . Defective understanding may [lead to] erroneous opinions . . . and these may in turn lead to false judgments and a wrong bias in the affections.
5. It is not immunity from temptation or the susceptibility to sin. . . . Our Lord was tempted in all points as we are, and yet He was without sin."[3]

How, then, with our human weaknesses, can we achieve this kind of "Christian perfection"?
- In character—Strive to become more and more like Christ.
- In holiness—Separate yourself from the world and its values; walk daily in the will of God; demonstrate God's love and mercy to others.
- In maturity—Work toward becoming more and more mature as a Christian—growing more Christlike, more holy and obedient in your daily walk.
- In love—Love others as God loves you.[4]

"Christian perfection . . . must be guarded by constant watchfulness, and maintained by divine grace. While we remain in this life, however deep our devotion, or fervent our religious life, there are sources of danger within us. . . . What Christian perfection does is to give grace to regulate these tendencies, affections, and passions, and bring them into subjection to the higher laws of human nature."[5]

Christian perfection "is not a triumph of human effort, but a work wrought in the heart by the Holy Spirit in answer to simple faith in the blood of Jesus."[6] It "consists solely in a life of perfect love, or the loving God with all the heart, soul, mind, and strength."[7] This was Paul's desire for the believers in the church at Corinth. There could be no unity with each other or with Paul unless these Corinthians would strive for perfection, until they would grow up into Christ and take care of their problems. Christian perfection is God's desire and His will for you and me, for your church and for mine.

God chose us in Christ Jesus *before the creation of the world to be holy and blameless in his sight* (Ephesians 1:4). It is the indwelling presence of the Holy Spirit in our lives that empowers us to grow into maturity in Christ.

6. Hebrews 6:1 says, *Leave the elementary teachings about Christ and go on to maturity.* List some disciplines that enable you to do that.

7. Record Paul's words in Philippians 3:12.

And if you press on, be confident of this: *that he who began a good work in you will carry it on to completion until the day of Jesus Christ* (Philippians 1:6).

> O to be like Thee! O to be like Thee,
>   Blessed Redeemer, pure as Thou art!
> Come in Thy sweetness; come in Thy fullness,
>   Stamp Thine own image deep on my heart.
> —Thomas O. Chisholm

May the God of peace . . . equip you with everything good for doing his will, and may he work in us what is pleasing to him, through Jesus Christ, to whom be glory forever and ever. Amen. (Hebrews 13:20-21).

MEMORY CHALLENGE

Read Philippians 2:5-11. Thank Jesus for His obedience and His shed blood on the Cross, which provided the means of our salvation. Sing a song of praise to Jesus.

DAY FIVE

Be of One Mind, Live in Peace

Read 2 Corinthians 13:11.

Paul hoped that instead of talking and arguing, the Corinthians would listen to him and to the Lord. (The *New American Standard Bible* translates *listen to my appeal* as *be comforted*, which would occur as a result of the encouragement that would come through obedience to Paul's appeal.)

1. What promise did Paul give the Corinthians if they would *aim for perfection* and unity in their church?

Be of one mind and live in peace are closely related. Unless there is unity in the church, it is not possible to *live in peace* with one another. It "does not mean that we all agree on everything, but that we agree not to disagree over matters that are not essential."[1]

Differences of opinion are inevitable and can even be helpful—if we agree that when we disagree, it will be in a loving manner and with a Christlike spirit. But *spiritual* agreement is essential; there must be unity of loyalty, commitment, and love for God and His Word. The church at Corinth was far from being unified in commitment to the truth of the gospel (11:4), and they were not living in peace with one another if, as Paul feared, they had not repented (12:20).

Spiritual gifts were a source of dissension in the Corinthian church (1 Corinthians 12). In his first letter to them, Paul compared the Body of Christ to the human body and explained that *the body is a unit, though it is made up of many parts; and though all its parts are many, they form one body* (verse 12). *God has combined the members of the body . . . so that there should be no division in the body, but that its parts should have equal concern for each other* (verse 24-25).

2. Another concern that Paul had addressed concerned the divisive factions in the church (1 Corinthians 1:11-12). What was Paul's appeal in 1 Corinthians 1:10?

3. What do the following verses tell us about church unity?

Psalm 133:1

Romans 12:16 (also found in 1 Peter 3:8)

Ephesians 4:3

4. Summarize Romans 15:5-6.

5. In Jesus' prayer for His disciples (John 17), what did He ask God three times to do for His disciples and for those *who will believe in me through their message* (verses 11, 21-22)?

According to verse 23, for what reason did Jesus ask that we be *brought to complete unity*?

6. If the church is *of one mind*, then it is able to *live in peace*. What do the following verses tell us about living in peace?

Psalm 34:14 (also found in 1 Peter 3:11)

Romans 14:17—The kingdom of God is

Colossians 3:15

7. We cannot *live in peace* in the Body of Christ unless we have peace in our own lives. *My peace I give you*, Jesus told us (John 14:27). Record Romans 5:1.

Paul said that the mind controlled by the Spirit is

_____ _____ _____ (Romans 8:6).

"True peace is not found in positive thinking, in absence of conflict, or in good feelings. It comes from knowing that God is in control"[2] and knowing that you belong to God.

May *the peace of God, which transcends all understanding . . . guard your hearts and your minds in Christ Jesus* (Philippians 4:7).

MEMORY CHALLENGE

Tell at least one person today about God's *indescribable gift*, Jesus Christ, and what He means to you.

DAY SIX

Giving God's Way

What an incredible journey Paul has guided us on as he has shared with us his words of concern and love for the church he founded in Corinth! Much in the same way as a beautiful thread might be woven in and out of a tapestry, the message of generous giving is woven throughout 2 Corinthians.

Paul had given the Corinthians the gift of the good news of Christ Jesus (Acts 18:1-18), and he gave it to them freely. He had supported himself as a tentmaker so that he might not be a burden to them (2 Corinthians 11:7). He gave them his time, even losing sleep in order to be available to minister to them and yet support himself (11:27). He gave himself; physically, he was afflicted, beaten, jailed, hungry, faced with difficult hardships, and he very nearly gave his life in order to take the gospel to the Gentiles (11:23-27). He prayed for them (13:7) and gave them his love (11:11).

Paul talked about the generosity of the Macedonians. They gave generously and cheerfully, despite their own poverty, to the believers in Jerusalem and also supplied any needs that Paul might have as he ministered to other congregations (8:1-5; 11:9). He gave us the most complete instructions in Scripture on God's plan and His grace for giving in His name (8—9).

And Paul told us about the greatest gift of all, the incomparable gift of God—redemption and eternal life, available through the shed blood of His Son, Jesus Christ, who gave His life for us. *Thanks be to God for his indescribable gift!* (2 Corinthians 9:15).

The Memory Challenge for this series of lessons in 2 Corinthians has been 2 Corinthians 9:6-15. Try to fill in the blanks without referring to your lessons or your Bible.

Remember this: Whoever _____ sparingly will also _____ sparingly, and whoever sows _____ will also reap _____. Each man should _____ what he has _____ in his _____ to _____, not _____ or under _____, for God loves a _____ _____. And God is _____ to make all _____ abound to you, so that in _____ _____ at _____ _____, having _____ that you _____, you will _____ in every _____ _____.

As it is written: "He has _____ abroad his _____ to the _____; his _____ endures _____."

Now he who _____ _____ to the _____ and _____ for _____ will also _____ and _____ your store of _____ and will _____ the _____ of your _____. You will be made _____ in _____ way so that you can be _____ on _____ _____, and through us _____ _____ will result in _____ to God.

This _____ that you perform is not only _____ the _____ of God's _____ but is also _____ in many _____ of _____ to _____. Because of the _____ by which you have _____ _____, men will _____ _____ for the _____ that accompanies your _____ of the _____ of Christ, and for your _____ in _____ with them and with _____ else. And in their _____ for you their _____ will go out to you, because of the _____ _____ God has _____ you. Thanks be to _____ for his _____ _____!

2 Corinthians 9:6-15

May the grace of the Lord Jesus Christ, and the love of God, and the fellowship of the Holy Spirit be with you all (2 Corinthians 13:14).

Notes

Introduction
    1. William Barclay, *The Daily Bible Study Series: Letters to the Corinthians*, rev. ed. (Philadelphia: Westminster Press, 1975), 1-2.
    2. Ibid., xiv.

Lesson 1, Day 2
    1. *Life Application Bible, New International Version* (Wheaton, Ill.: Tyndale House Publishers; and Grand Rapids: Zondervan Publishing House, 1991), 2093.
    2. William MacDonald, *Believer's Bible Commentary* (Thomas Nelson Publishers, 1995, 1993, 1990, 1989), 1820.

Lesson 1, Day 3
    1. Barclay, *The Daily Bible Study Series: Letters to the Corinthians*, 172.
    2. Ibid., 173.

Lesson 2, Day 1
    1. Frank G. Carver, *Beacon Bible Commentary, Corinthians* (Kansas City: Beacon Hill Press of Kansas City, 1968), 518.
    2. Rick Warren, *The Purpose-Driven Life* (Grand Rapids: Zondervan Publishing House, 2002), 97.

Lesson 2, Day 4
    1. *Life Application Bible, New International Version*, 2284.

Lesson 2, Day 5
    1. Barclay, *The Daily Bible Study Series: Letters to the Corinthians*, 197.

Lesson 2, Day 6
    1. Warren, *The Purpose-Driven Life*, 273.
    2. *Life Application Bible Commentary: 1 and 2 Corinthians* (Wheaton, Ill.: Tyndale House Publishers, Copyright 1999 by The Livingstone Corporation), 331.

Lesson 3, Day 2
    1. *Life Application Bible Commentary: 1 and 2 Corinthians*, 342.

Lesson 3, Day 3
    1. Carver, *Beacon Bible Commentary, Corinthians*, 547.
    2. Warren, *The Purpose-Driven Life*, 228.

Lesson 3, Day 4
    1. Barclay, *The Daily Bible Study Series: Letters to the Corinthians*, 208.
    2. *Life Application Bible, New International Version*, 2099.

Lesson 3, Day 5
    1. Madeleine S. Miller and J. Lane Miller, *Harper's Bible Dictionary* (New York: Harper and Brothers Publishers, 1952, 1954), 603-4.
    2. Ibid., 605.
    3. *Webster's New World College Dictionary*, 4th ed., s.v. "ambassador."

Lesson 3, Day 6
    1. *Life Application Bible, New International Version*, 2100.
    2. Barclay, *The Daily Bible Study Series: Letters to the Corinthians*, 212.
    3. Alan Redpath, *Blessings Out of Buffetings: Studies in 2 Corinthians* (Westwood, N.J.: Fleming H. Revell, 1965), 112.

Lesson 4, Day 1
    1. "Graham's Class 'Act'—He Practices What He Preaches," *Daily Oklahoman*, June 12, 2003, 6A.
    2. "Berry Tramel: A Role Model for Athletes," *Daily Oklahoman*, June 12, 2003, 1C, 3C.

Lesson 4, Day 2
    1. Barclay, *The Daily Bible Study Series: Letters to the Corinthians*, 212-13.
    2. Special Photo Issue, 2002, The Voice of the Martyrs, P.O. Box 443, Bartlesville, OK 74005.
    3. Ibid.
    4. Ibid.
    5. Ibid.
    6. Barclay, *The Daily Bible Study Series: Letters to the Corinthians*, 215.

Lesson 4, Day 3
    1. Barclay, *The Daily Bible Study Series: Letters to the Corinthians*, 560.

Lesson 4, Day 4
    1. *Reader's Digest Great Encyclopedic Dictionary* (Pleasantville, N.Y.: The Reader's Digest Association, 1966), 977.
    2. *Life Application Bible, New International Version*, 2242.

Lesson 4, Day 5
    1. *Life Application Bible, New International Version*, 2100.

Lesson 4, Day 6
    1. Carver, *Beacon Bible Commentary, Corinthians*, 564.

Lesson 5, Day 1
    1. *Reader's Digest Great Encyclopedic Dictionary*, 1094.
    2. Miller and Miller, *Harper's Bible Dictionary*, 264-65.
    3. Adam Clarke, *Clarke's Commentary*, vol. 6 (New York and Nashville: Abingdon Press, 1977), 344.
    4. H. Orton Wiley and Paul T. Culbertson, *Introduction to Christian Theology* (Kansas City: Beacon Hill Press, 1947), 298.

Lesson 5, Day 2
    1. Miller and Miller, *Harper's Bible Dictionary*, 609.
    2. Ibid.
    3. Charles Hodge, *The Crossway Classic Commentaries: 2 Corinthians* (Wheaton, Ill.: Crossway Books, 1995), 146.

Lesson 5, Day 3
    1. Colin Kruse, *The Second Epistle of Paul to the Corinthians* (Grand Rapids: Wm. B. Eerdmans Publishing Co., 1987), 147.

Lesson 5, Day 4
    1. J. Vernon McGee, *Thru the Bible Commentary Series, Second Corinthians* (Nashville: Thomas Nelson Publishers, 1975, 1991), 97.
    2. *Life Application Bible, New International Version*, 388.

Lesson 5, Day 5
    1. Henry Snyder Gehman, ed., *The New Westminster Dictionary of the Bible* (Philadelphia: Westminster Press, 1976), 421.

Lesson 5, Day 6
    1. Carver, *Beacon Bible Commentary, Corinthians*, 581.

Lesson 6, Day 1
    1. Gehman, *The New Westminster Dictionary of the Bible*, 405.
    2. Warren W. Wiersbe, *Be Encouraged* (Colorado Springs: Chariot Victor Publishing, 1984), 101.

Lesson 6, Day 3
    1. Barclay, *The Daily Bible Study Series: Letters to the Corinthians*, 238.

Lesson 6, Day 5
    1. Hodge, *The Crossway Classic Commentaries: 2 Corinthians*, 84.
    2. Ibid.

Lesson 6, Day 6

1. *Life Application Bible Commentary: 1 and 2 Corinthians*, 417.
2. Wiersbe, *Be Encouraged*, 110.

Lesson 7, Day 1

1. Barclay, *The Daily Bible Study Series: Letters to the Corinthians*, 242-43.
2. J. B. Chapman, *Bud Robinson, A Brother Beloved* (Kansas City: Beacon Hill Press, 1943), 33.
3. *Life Story of Bud Robinson* (Cincinnati, Oh.: Revivalist Press), 33.
4. Chapman, *Bud Robinson*, 34.
5. Ibid., 63.
6. Ibid., 12.
7. Ibid., 63.

Lesson 7, Day 2

1. Wiersbe, *Be Encouraged*, 112.

Lesson 7, Day 3

1. Carver, *Beacon Bible Commentary, Corinthians*, 596.

Lesson 7, Day 4

1. Carver, *Beacon Bible Commentary, Corinthians*, 600.
2. *Life Application Bible Commentary: 1 and 2 Corinthians* (Grand Rapids: William B. Eerdmans Publishing Co., 1965), 428.
3. Colin Kruse, *Tyndale New Testament Commentaries: 2 Corinthians*, 183. [Credit for material in this paragraph not in quotes goes to P. Batey, *Paul's Bride Image: A Symbol of Realistic Eschatology* (1963), 176-82.]

Lesson 7, Day 5

1. *Life Application Bible, New International Version*, 2192.

Lesson 8, Day 1

1. *Life Application Bible Commentary: 1 and 2 Corinthians*, 433.
2. Ibid.

Lesson 8, Day 2

1. *Daily Oklahoman*, January 3, 2004, Opinion Page (14A).

Lesson 8, Day 3

1. *Life Application Bible, New International Version*, 1870.

Lesson 8, Day 4

1. *Life Application Bible, New International Version*, 1792.

Lesson 8, Day 6

1. Donna Behrke-White, "Students Show Hunger for Religious Knowledge," *Miami Herald*, quoted in *Daily Oklahoman*, January 3, 2004, Opinion Page (14A).
2. Wiley and Culbertson, *Introduction to Christian Theology*, 220.
3. Ibid., 221.

Lesson 9, Day 1

1. Based on information from *Life Application Bible Commentary*, 435-37, and *Life Application Bible, New International Version*, 2209.

Lesson 9, Day 2

1. James M. Scott, *New International Biblical Commentary: 1 and 2 Corinthians* (Peabody, Mass.: Hendrickson Publishers, 1998), 214.
2. Carver, *Beacon Bible Commentary: Corinthians*, 610.
3. *Life Application Bible Commentary: 1 and 2 Corinthians*, 440.

Lesson 9, Day 3

1. Hodge, *The Crossway Classic Commentaries: 2 Corinthians*, 213.
2. Wiersbe, *Be Encouraged*, 130.

Lesson 9, Day 4

1. Wiersbe, *Be Encouraged*, 135.
2. Ibid., 136.

Lesson 9, Day 5

1. *Life Application Bible, New International Version*, 2109.

Lesson 9, Day 6

1. Carver, *Beacon Bible Commentary: Corinthians*, 631.
2. Wiersbe, *Be Encouraged*, 145.

Lesson 10, Day 1

1. Carver, *Beacon Bible Commentary: Corinthians*, 639.
2. *Life Application Bible Commentary: 1 and 2 Corinthians*, 465.

Lesson 10, Day 2

1. Carver, *Beacon Bible Commentary: Corinthians*, 641.

Lesson 10, Day 3

1. *Life Application Bible, New International Version*, 2110.
2. *New International Biblical Commentary: 2 Corinthians*, 261.

Lesson 10, Day 4

1. Carver, *Beacon Bible Commentary, Corinthians*, 643.
2. *Life Application Bible, New International Version*, 2234.
3. Wiley and Culbertson, *Introduction to Christian Theology*, 325-26.
4. Adapted from *Life Application Bible, New International Version*, 1656.
5. Wiley and Culbertson, *Introduction to Christian Theology*, 327.
6. Ibid.
7. Ibid., 328.

Lesson 10, Day 5

1. Wiersbe, *Be Encouraged*, 151.
2. *Life Application Bible, New International Version*, 2153.